ARCTIC OCEAN

NEW SIBERIAN ISLANDS

EAST SIBERIAN SEA

BERING SEA

ORTH LAND

LAPTEV SEA

RA SEA

KAMCHATKA

Lena

SEA OF OKHOTSK

SIBERIA

Yenisey

SAKHALIN

Angara

VOSIBIRSK

Lake Baykal

Irkutsk ●

SEA OF JAPAN

AINS

MONGOLIA

NORTH KOREA

JAPAN

SOUTH
KOREA

YELLOW SEA

CHINA

THE SOVIET UNION

| 0 | 800 miles |
| 0 | 1200 km |

USTINOV
IN RUSSIA

**DRAWINGS BY PETER USTINOV
PHOTOGRAPHS BY
PETER USTINOV AND JOHN McGREEVY**

USTINOV
IN RUSSIA

SUMMIT BOOKS
New York

First published in Great Britain, 1987
by Michael O'Mara Books Limited,
20 Queen Anne Street, London W1N 9FB

Published by SUMMIT BOOKS
A Division of Simon & Schuster, Inc
Simon & Schuster Building, Rockefeller Center
1230 Avenue of the Americas, New York, NY 10020

SUMMIT BOOKS and colophon are trademarks of
Simon & Schuster, Inc

Edited by Clare Pumfrey
Designed by Martin Bristow

Typeset by V & M Graphics Limited, Aylesbury, Bucks
Printed and bound in West Germany by Mohndruck, Gütersloh

10 9 8 7 6 5 4 3 2 1

ISBN 0–671–65954–5

The television series from which this book is drawn was produced and
directed by John McGreevy in association with CTV Television
Network and with the participation of Telefilm Canada.

The author would like to thank Michael Foss without whose help
this book would have been impossible.

CONTENTS

AN HISTORICAL OUTLINE

9th century A Russian state centred on Kiev emerged from a collection of Slavic tribes. The Varangians, a tribe of Viking origin, took power and provided the first ruler, Rurik. A Viking trade route stretched from the Baltic Sea, through Novgorod and Kiev to Constantinople. Kiev was the capital, founded by a Viking chief, Ki.

971 During Sviatoslav's reign, the 4th prince, the new state was invaded by the Pechenegs. The Polovtsians, another tribe, managed to cut Russia off from the Black Sea.

988 Byzantine Christianity was adopted by Vladimir I (980–1015) of Kiev. At this time, Kiev became one of the largest and finest cities in Europe.

End of 11th century Kiev fell into decline, later coming under Polish-Lithuanian control. In 1169 the capital was transferred to Vladimir. There was no united state as such, but a collection of rival principalities, the most important of which were Vladimir-Suzdal and Novgorod. The latter was unique in having an elected prince and a *veche*, or city council, and it was a prosperous trading city. Feuds between the principalities led to invasions from Swedes, Germans, Lithuanians, Poles and Turks.

1230s Invasion by the Tartars, or Mongols, from the east. In 1240 Kiev was destroyed and the Russian principalities were invaded and subjugated to the empire of the Golden Horde. Novgorod alone, under Alexander Nevsky, remained unoccupied.

1380 The battle of Kulikovo saw the first defeat of the Tartars by Prince Dmitri of Moscow, and in 1480 Ivan III (the Great) of Moscow renounced the Tartar yoke. He annexed the territories of other principalities, including Novgorod, and expanded against the Tartars to the south and east. Moscow became the centre of this expanding Russian state.

1533–84 Ivan IV (the Terrible) pushed forward the frontiers to include Astrakhan and much of Siberia. He instituted a strong centralised autocracy and a secret police force, the *oprichnina*.

1598–1613 Known as the Time of Troubles, follows the end of the Rurik dynasty. Boris Godunov became Regent in 1598 for the feeble-minded surviving son of Ivan IV, Fyodor. Godunov proclaimed himself Tsar when Fyodor died. He believed that he could found a dynasty with the help of the Church.

1613 Mikhail Romanov was elected Tsar and power was restored. Moscow became the undisputed capital.

17th century A period of both expansion and crisis with uprisings and religious problems. Serfdom developed and in 1649 it was decreed that peasants were forbidden to move from the estates of their lords. A schism occurred in the Orthodox Church, with the 'Old Believers' opposing religious reform.

Peter the Great (1682–1725) founded St. Petersburg to replace Moscow as the capital in 1703. His reign was notable for his ruthless programme of modernisation which aroused strong opposition. He conquered parts of the Baltic coast and created a 'window on the west'. A policy of westernisation was enforced by the power of the central government, and by fully developing serfdom and creating a service nobility. Peter's wars against the Swedes and the Turks turned Russia into a European power. Expansion into Siberia continued and the Russians had reached the Bering Straits when Peter died. They went on to colonise Alaska and the coast of California.

Catherine the Great (1762–96) pursued Peter's policies of westernisation, expanding them into the cultural and educational fields. Expansion policy continued through the partitions of Poland and the defeat of the Turks. The Crimea was annexed, the shores of the Black Sea controlled and large areas of the Ukraine conquered.

Alexander I (1801–25) discussed plans for political reform along western lines but these were not carried through. Russia's success against Napoleon made her a major force in European diplomacy. Finland, the Duchy of Poland and large areas of the Caucasus became part of the Empire. Despite its apparent growth in power, a situation was developing which was ripe for revolution. The division between social groups – high officials, landowners and those that worked the land – was exaggerated as time went on.

1825 The Decembrist uprising of noble army officers calling for Western political reform failed and Nicholas I reacted by turning away from the West.

1853–6 The Crimean War. British and French troops invaded the Crimea in reaction to Nicholas I's Turkish policy.

Alexander II (1855–81) was known as the Liberator Tsar because he freed the serfs and initiated other reforms. He introduced *Zemstvos*, which were provincial assemblies which sorted out local issues. He started Russia's social and economic transformation. It appeared to be the start of a new era, but it was short-lived. A revolutionary movement, inspired by Western anarchist and socialist ideas, the populists, assassinated him in 1881.

1880s–1890s Under Alexander III (1881–1894) and Nicholas II (1894–1917) expansion into Central Asia continued, even as far as the borders of China, Persia and Afghanistan. At the same time, state-sponsored industrialisation was accelerated. A Marxist movement developed in exile.

1904–5 Russo-Japanese war ending in humiliating defeat for Russia.

1914 Russia enters World War I, leading to the fall of the Romanov dynasty in February 1917. It was replaced by a Provisional government aiming at a liberal constitutional régime.

October 1917 Bolshevik Revolution under Lenin.

1918–20 Civil war between the Whites and the new Red government. The White armies were assisted by European powers and Japan, USA and Canada.

1921 Introduction of the New Economic Policy and the Kronstadt rebellion. The USSR was finally constituted by 1924, the year of Lenin's death. Stalin was in power by 1928.

1928–31 The first Five Year Plan. Rapid, forced industrialisation and collectivisation of agriculture followed by mass purges in the 1930s.

1939 Nazi-Soviet Pact. Nazis invade Russia in June 1941. After the battle of Stalingrad the Red army advanced to the west and entered Berlin. After 1947–8 the war-time alliance between Russia and the West was replaced by the Cold War and Soviet régimes were established throughout Eastern Europe.

1953 Death of Stalin.

1956 Krushchev's secret speech denounced Stalin's crimes. Krushchev initiated reforms, ended the purges and restored the primacy of the party over one-man rule. He was ousted in 1964 and replaced by Brezhnev and Kosygin who followed more cautious policies.

March 1985 Mikhail Gorbachev was elected first secretary of the party.

The great palace at Petrodvorets, near Leningrad (top), was built as a summer residence for Peter the Great. From the terrace a dramatic cascade of water, including 64 fountains and decorated with 255 gilded bronze statues (right), descends to a pool. The stone figure of Saturn eating one of his children (left) stands in a Leningrad garden.

CHAPTER ONE

BY WAY OF NO APOLOGY

I am a Russian of a kind. Though I was born in London and I am a British citizen, I was conceived in Leningrad, and let no one tell me this is without importance. I am neither white nor red, but, whether I wish it or not, a part of me belongs to that great and mysterious land. What I am now cannot be divorced from a past that gave a form to my genes. I am a man in the middle, and content with my lot.

The name Ustinov is Russian. My father's grandfather went to Siberia when he was young, engaged in some business to do with salt-mines, and returned to Leningrad extremely wealthy and the owner of an immense amount of land. At the time of his death, the archives mention the construction of 16 churches and the possession of 6,000 serfs. My mother's father became court architect to the Tsar and, later, the first President of the Soviet Academy of Fine Arts. When he died, in 1928, his valedictory included Mozart's Requiem and a state funeral. He is buried in the Moscow cemetery of Novodevichi, in notorious company.

Many members of my mother's family are still living in Leningrad. When I was making my television film series there, my first cousins suddenly arrived with a present of strawberries and cream; a large amount of the most succulent strawberries buried under a mound of the most delicious cream. This touching gift pleased me particularly because the strawberries had been gathered, with much affection and no little labour, in the grounds of my grandfather's old dacha, out by the Baltic shore.

Reverence, affection, sentiment: are these not among the finer qualities of humanity? I have found that the Russians have extraordinary feelings for their land and their past.

A friend of mine in Paris, a photographer of Russian origin and the son of a famous church bass, decided to visit his unknown homeland. His mother threw up her hands in distress (as, indeed, did mine when I first went), but since she could not prevent her son from going, she asked him to bring back a little soil from the ancestral town of Tver so she could scatter it on her husband's grave in Paris. The son made the icy, winter journey and descended from the train at Tver. To dig up some earth, he had to scrape away the snow first. As he was doing this, he heard the pounding of heavy feet approaching. His collar was seized by a guard with a machine-gun who demanded, ominously, why my friend was taking liberties with state property. When the reason for the digging was explained, the guard thrust his machine-gun into my friend's hands, fell to his knees in the snow, and vigorously attacked the earth. He wrapped the soil carefully in some newspaper, and tied it nice and tight. Then he briskly exchanged this parcel for his gun and continued his stern stewardship of the Soviet present, while my friend returned to Paris with the soil of Holy Russia, wrapped in a copy of *Izvestiya*.

The land and the past are like the steadying sails of reassurance to the Russians. So often the emigré, who is deprived of them, finds himself at an odd disadvantage in the world outside. He finds it hard to set a safe course.

Once, in New York, I was visited in the theatre by a thin, sallow man in an old, old raincoat; a figure so miserable and dejected that he might well have come straight from a concentration camp. He hovered at the stage door, mumbling inaudibly, and ran away when I asked him in.

The next day, as I was going to the theatre, he came up to me in Times Square. He preferred to talk in the midst of people and had been frightened to see me alone. He was a clown, he said. A Jewish clown from Soviet Georgia.

'Very funny clown,' he said. 'Good notices somewhere.' No, he'd left them in his other trousers. But he'd been on television back home.

'Well,' I said, 'what can I do to help you?'

'The sound of laughter,' he replied. 'It needs me, the sound of laughter.'

'But what are you doing at the moment?'

A jet of water shoots 25 metres up into the air from a statue of Samson tearing open the jaws of a lion. A long canal, crossed by ornamental bridges, runs from the bottom of the cascade to a small harbour on the Gulf of Finland.

Red Square, Moscow. The magnificent Cathedral of the Intercession, St. Basil's, was built for Ivan the Terrible, who is said to have blinded the architects so that no comparable building could be designed.

'I am doing very well. No need for money. I'm cutting the hair of men in St. Regis Hotel.'

'So you are a barber too?' I said.

'No,' he replied, 'I am doing what I remember from the old Chaplin pictures.'

'My God,' I cried, 'don't your clients worry about that?'

He shrugged. 'No, they are very nice people. They read their papers, they're not interested in what I'm doing. They leave good tips and I am very well off. I am just a single man here.'

He paused. His face, sad in animation, became tragic as he formulated his thoughts.

'But still,' he said at last, 'it misses me, the sound of laughter. It is possible that in Russia there is a little persecution. But you know, Mr Ustinov, it is better than neglect.'

For the Westerner, any journey to the Soviet Union is a step into the unknown. There are so many extraordinary reports, so many contradictory stories. The weight of centuries of prejudice burdens his shoulders; his head is stuffed up with the poisonous fogs of the Cold War – all the Cold Wars. It's extraordinary how Russia is invariably the potential enemy in peace time. In war, she becomes an ally of vital importance. Then, once peace breaks out, she reverts to being a potential enemy again almost immediately .

When I went to Moscow in 1985, with my Canadian partners, to tie up the details of our project, I took with me the familiar doubts and fears. We had an interview with the then Minister of Culture, Mr Demichev, and he asked us what we wanted to do. I told him roughly what we had in mind: a free and pragmatic adaptation of my book on Russian history, with photography from various parts of the Soviet Union which we would select and edit to our liking. The representative held up a peremptory hand and immediately declared, 'It's useless for this conversation to go any further.'

We looked at each other anxiously. Were we staring at hopelessness and defeat already? Was this the authoritarian, closed Russia that we had been led to expect? But then the Minister continued. 'We appreciate your work and, more importantly, we trust you. As far as my Ministry is concerned, you have a *carte blanche* throughout the Soviet Union.'

This happened before Gorbachev and *glasnost*, and the Ministry was as good as its word. We went on our way, free to make our film in our own manner, and subject only to the petty pin-pricks of bureaucracy that are a well-known feature of so many lands, and so many governments. We had our little difficulties with airlines, with freight, with schedules, but who has not been subject to these trials the world over? On the one occasion when some jack-in-office tried to forbid us to film, I demanded to talk directly to Mr Demichev at the Ministry. The prohibition was withdrawn at once. I noticed that the people were as hospitable as they were officious, but also, that clear instructions coming from high places were very rigorously adhered to.

There we were, a small, compact Western production company, moving fast and lightly across the face of the land. In places unused to strangers, we obviously became objects of interest and curiosity. We had two Russians attached to our party and they were not, as the common myth would have it, spies and guardians, but rather administrators and invaluable helpers, and they smoothed our way very effectively. We were received with charm and grace almost everywhere, though perhaps with surprise too, and we also had our share of sticky moments. In Moscow, in a famous gallery, we came up against one of those administrators who derive too much evident pleasure from a position of authority. Why must we photograph the actual pictures when reproductions of the paintings already exist? Why must we film that painting of Mussorgsky when it obviously showed the poor fellow saturated in drink and near death? She was of a type that is irksome to deal with and almost impossible to placate, but with patience, persistence and some help from our Russian companions we persuaded her to allow us to photograph two rooms.

When we had finished, I made a point of thanking her profusely for her great kindness. She accepted my gratitude in good grace, perhaps because she was unaware of the great kindness I was referring to. At least I am sure that she understood that our intentions were serious and sympathetic, and not the usual attempts to score gratuitous points in a propaganda war. Whether her change of attitude extended to her next client I cannot, however, guarantee.

I was reminded of this episode when the American Company CBS wanted to shoot us shooting for their excellent programme 'Sixty Minutes'. The Russians, with their habitual mistrust of Western journalists, refused to allow the CBS team entry into the Soviet Union. We eventually prevailed upon them to change their minds, arguing that any publicity was good in the West, and that even health warnings made inveterate smokers think of cigarettes. That experienced investigative journalist Morley Safer was selected to question me.

His very first question in the amicable inquisition set the tone for what followed.

'Peter, can you work here *at all*, you, who have known the freedom of the United States?'

I replied that I found the question difficult to answer in that form, since a play of mine, on tour in the United States, had enjoyed every kind of privilege, and, indeed, freedom, until the day it opened in the provinces. Then opinions were democratically divided as to what was wrong with it. The backers and the producers impressed on me the extent of their investment, and under that kind of pressure, I made certain changes against my better judgment. Miraculously it ran for as long as six weeks in New York.

Meanwhile, without my knowing it, the Russians had got hold of the script, and for them, once the script is accepted, the author's intentions are sacrosanct. Ironically, the day before the interview with Mr Safer, I had been at a matinée of the same play, celebrating the tenth anniversary with the cast. Ten years in repertory represents over a year's run in a big city. 'It's wonderful for an author to see his work as he wrote it,' I told Mr Safer. 'And to me, that is part of freedom.'

Needless to say, that part of the interview was not included in the finished programme.

At Zagorsk, the Canterbury of the Russian Orthodox Church, we were invited to lunch in the Seminary by the Director. In the course of a convivial and cheerful meal, he filled our glasses with vodka. Then, rising to his feet, he proposed a toast to Soviet–American friendship. This nicety of super-power protocol over, we went on with the inevitable small talk until the Metropolitan filled the glasses again, and rose to toast 'Continued Soviet-American friendship.'

I turned uneasily to John McGreevy, the producer, and asked, 'Does he know we are not American?'

'I shouldn't bother to bring that up now,' he said.

'What happens if he finds out? Won't he feel we've made a fool of him?'

I decided to tell him the truth, in this *place* of truth.

'You know, Your Eminence – '

He lent me his ear, smiling engagingly.

' – we are not American.'

The Trinity and St. Sergius Monastery at Zagorsk is the largest monastery in the country and a centre of pilgrimage. The Church of the Holy Spirit, 1476, (top left), and the Cathedral of the Dormition, 1559–85, (above and top right) with its five enormous blue and gold domes. Pilgrims come to drink the holy water in the small painted chapel outside.

The Cathedral of the Dormition and the Church of the Holy Spirit, Zagorsk (top). The Cathedral of the Trinity (above) contains the body of St. Sergius who founded the monastery.

The smile faded abruptly. He fixed me with blue eyes which tended to water.

'What are you?' he demanded.

'This is a Canadian unit.'

'Canadian … ' he murmured, as though trying to place it in his mind's eye. He refilled the glasses, a little carelessly. He rose and toasted Soviet-Canadian friendship. Then he sat, and smiled at me, his cheeks slightly flushed.

'From what part of Canada do you come?' he inquired.

'Me? Oh I'm not Canadian,' I said.

'*Not* Canadian?' he cried, as though such a thing defied credibility. 'What are you?'

'British.'

'British,' he echoed, in horror. Then he filled the glasses again, spilling a little on the tablecloth.

He rose and toasted Anglo-Soviet friendship.

He sat down again, giggling, and deduced, between laughs, that at least all the rest of us were Canadian.

'No,' I said truthfully, 'our cameraman is Icelandic.'

'Is what?' the Metropolitan hissed.

'Icelandic.'

He tried to concentrate on his task. He refilled the glasses. This time rather more vodka landed on the tablecloth.

He rose, a little out of breath, high in colour.

'I propose a toast,' he muttered, 'to Soviet– ...'

He inclined his head in my direction.

'Icelandic,' I prompted.

He closed his eyes.

'What?' he snapped.

'Icelandic.'

'Icelandic friendship.'

He sank back rather than sat down. I did not have the heart to tell him of John McGreevy's Irish origins.

When we were preparing for our Russian adventure, working from Canada, telexes whizzed between us and Moscow. We would dictate our queries to those pretty secretaries of the New World, those placid, serene girls with pearly teeth and freckles, and an alarming ignorance of other times, other lands and other peoples. 'Send supplementary information on Lenin,' we dictated. This, inevitably, became: 'Send supplementary information on Lennon.' Next day, back came the answer: 'We do not understand why you ask us about Lennon. Suggest you call Yoko Ono.'

The Cathedral of the Annunciation in the Kremlin, Moscow (1484–9). The elaborately decorated exterior was mostly added by Ivan the Terrible who also built four chapels and two additional gilded domes. After his excommunication he built a small chamber with a separate entrance, where he could listen to the service in the cathedral without being in the church itself.

The Winter Palace, Leningrad, which houses the Hermitage Art Collection in some of its 1,500 rooms, was built between 1754 and 1764. In 1837 the interior was gutted by fire and then restored mostly in contemporary style. The magnificent Jordan staircase (far left) leads from the ground floor to the Tsars' apartments. It is made of Carrara marble with polished granite columns on the first floor. Its name derives from an annual ceremony when the Tsars went down the staircase to bless the waters of the River Neva, in commemoration of the baptism of Christ. The Pavilion Hall (above) was rebuilt after the fire in place of six of the original rooms. It is among the grandest rooms in the palace with white fluted columns, pale pink marble walls and crystal chandeliers. The Raphaelesque loggia (left) in the Hermitage.

A view into Red Square beyond the Beklemishev tower on the left (top left), and the walls of the Kremlin, with St. Basil's in the distance; looking down the River Moskva (top right) with the fortified walls and towers of the Kremlin on the right; fishermen on the banks of the Moskva; the Kremlin Cathedrals, with the bell-tower built by Ivan the Great.

The Russians are extraordinarily alive to the West, its fads and fancies, its novelties and nonsense. Even in modest restaurants the pop music is quite deafening, so loud in fact that the waiter's voice, telling you that most of the items on the menu are off, is drowned out. Ordering a meal has to be done in mime, all the more difficult because the strobe-lights give the impression that the entire transaction is on silent film. The ocean is full of surf-boards and pedalos, and many public lavatories have very noisy hot-air machines for drying your hands. In Siberia, a land associated with endless snows and unbearable cold, large buildings are often studded with air-conditioners, as they are in New York. The heat in summer is often as arduous as the snow in winter.

The surprises are endless, as endless as the misapprehensions, the legends, and the distortions of the truth.

It is, obviously, in the interest of the media to dramatise the difference between peoples. Without that there is no conflict, no drama, no justification for the purchase of newspapers. But once we have accepted that differences do exist, are we not impressed, if we are honest with ourselves, by the great similarities between peoples? Is there not a unity in the composition of humanity? If a baby is crying next door, we cannot tell its colour or its race by the sound of its voice, its only means of expression. The raw material is the same until the prejudices of tradition begin to erode virgin sensibilities, and a particular view of history identifies long-standing enmities.

Education is responsible for necessary enlightenment, but also for the sediment of old saws and unquestioned imbecilities elaborated and refined since the dawn of civilisation.

This book is not an apology, nor is it a work of devil's advocacy. It is not my business to refute the prattle of politicians, or to point out their inexperience in spheres other than their own. I merely hope that this record of a particular mission covering some 20,000 miles within the Soviet Union will serve to stimulate the reader into questioning some of the things we are all asked to believe, and to reach conclusions about them which are, at least, personal.

The Novodevichi convent near Moscow was founded in 1524 to celebrate Vasili III's victory
in recapturing the old city of Smolensk. The Church of the Virgin of Smolensk (top)
is the principal church; the Refectory and Church of the Dormition (above left);
the Gate Church of the Transfiguration (above right).

CHAPTER TWO

TOWARDS COMPREHENSION

Three Russian proverbs:

'Love thy neighbour, but build a wall.'

'The road to the church is icy; so is the road to the tavern, but I will walk carefully.'

'When engaged in a fight, it is not the moment to part your hair.'

These are redolent of contradictions in the Russian character; an inherent religious fervour, tempered by a scepticism about human motives; a regard for protocol, and a sly avoidance of it; a bluff logic about there being a time and place for most things, good and bad.

It is obvious that both geography and climate play important parts in the formation of national character. Space and distance play havoc with concepts of time, and, therefore, with punctuality. Extreme heat and extreme cold also leave their impression on people, inducing volatility or slothfulness, or subtle blends of both.

Perhaps Ivan the Terrible was as eloquent about all this as anyone. We found him morosely meditating in the glacial medieval chapel in Novodevichi, his favourite haunt when consumed by contrition after dire and turbulent events.

'Your Majesty,' I said, somewhat nervously.

'Never mind the protocol,' he snapped impatiently, 'I have not long to live.'

He had been married six times. Never had he found a replacement for his first love, whom he affectionately called, 'My Little Heifer.'

I asked him why he had sent a delegation to the Court of Queen Elizabeth I, in order to find a seventh wife.

'We are surrounded by uncertainty,' he mused. 'The endless horizon is rich with unpleasant possibilities. In the east and south nomadic Asiatic tribes are perpetually on the move, as fierce and unpredictable as a force of nature. In the west, other eyes glance enviously in our direction, those of the Teutonic Knights and the marauding armies of the Catholic Kingdom of Poland, to say nothing

The magnificent brick bell-tower of the Novodevichi convent (1690); the domes of the bell-tower and the principal church; a detail of a fresco above the entrance to the Church of the Virgin of Smolensk; the fortified walls and towers of the convent, which was originally one of several fortress convents built to defend the capital.

of the Swedes. Only in the north do we confront the safety of the sea. It was an Englishman who first made a hole in our roof, through which the fresh air could reach our nostrils, even if that hole is covered by snow for most of the year. An Englishman.'

'Richard Chancellor.'

'Don't complicate the issue with foreign-sounding names. The Englishman!' he roared, and then regained his composure. 'It is for that reason that I searched for a wife in England. I hoped she might bring a little of the sea with her, even a whiff of brine ...'

And he fell into a melancholy reverie. He had just virtually destroyed the city of Novgorod, a unique case in Russian history. The city-state, north-west of Moscow, had traded with the West and become immensely wealthy. It had prospered with a republican form of self-government, a democracy of a sort, an unparalleled cultural and commercial centre, with territories stretching from the western borders of Russia to the confines of the habitable north. Now it lay in ruins.

'Novgorod had to learn that she was part of Russia. Russia is not Novgorod's garden,' he snarled.

'But they say the rivers ran red with blood,' I protested.

He became casual.

'Quite possible. When the body is ill the doctor lets blood. I am Russia's doctor.'

His eyes met mine.

'Death becomes a habit,' he said, 'like remorse. The two need one another.'

Since I found no ready answer to this, he went on, confidentially, almost whispering his confession.

'You know I killed my son?'

I said I had heard the rumour.

'Hit him on the head with my walking stick. What father hasn't done this at one time or other? How was I to know he had a thin skull?' He sighed. 'I console myself with the thought that, with all the low arches in the Kremlin, it would have happened sooner or later in any case ...'

As I left this mercurial fellow, with his uncontrollable rages and mixture of suspicion and superstition, who traced his lineage from Caesar Augustus with the help of some unreliable authorities, he murmured almost inaudibly, and with uncharacteristic generosity, 'I will pray for your soul, even though you are still alive ...'

Russia has never enjoyed the happy destiny of Western Europe, with its clearly defined frontiers, the Pyrenees, the Rhine, the Alps, and above all the sea, a sea without danger of invasion, a permanent invitation to adventure, El Dorado, the New World, Cathay ... Russia has merely an infinity of featureless land, the endless steppe, too vast and too formless for a fixed defence against unpredictable assault.

This very size, which seemed to the West both sinister and menacing, was in fact a terrible handicap. 'The Sleeping Giant' was the phrase coined to express the Western fear of Russia's potential, just as the 'Yellow Peril' became the racist cliché to express alarm at Chinese fecundity. Neither nation deserved their reputation, any more than King Kong, the monster with the golden heart, merited the fear and aggression of the crowd. Naturally, since the crowd was composed of people of normal size, they were less concerned with the big ape's motives, and more with where he put his feet, since he was quite capable of causing death by clumsiness. In the same way, Russia acquired a reputation for expansionism, mainly among those who were far better at it themselves.

At a time when such activities were still popular, and encouraged by the highest secular and spiritual authorities, relatively small nations such as the British, the French, the Spanish, the Portuguese, the Dutch and the Belgians, squabbled and scrapped over territories which belonged to none of them. Their ships roved the world with their cargo of conquistadors and prelates, eager to carry the bitter fruits of civilisation to the four corners of the earth. Germany and Italy had been slow to unify, and joined this particular game long after the umpire's whistle had blown to indicate that expansionism was no longer fashionable, or perhaps merely that the choicest morsels were firmly in the hands of club members, and there was

St. Basil's Cathedral, Red Square with its decorated domes silhouetted against the sky. The faceted onion domes are painted in brilliant primary colours.

The towers and domes of Novgorod. The town was founded in the 9th century on the system of lakes and rivers which carried trade from the Baltic to the Black Sea. It became a very powerful, independent republic with its own elected assembly. The Kremlin with its red brick ramparts stands on the banks of the River Volkhov.

nothing much left to take. They grabbed what they could, Namibia, Togo, Tanganyika, Libya, Samoa, Eritrea, Somalia and finally, briefly and very late in history, Ethiopia. The Germans, cheated of their colonial ambitions by the Treaty of Versailles after World War I, embarked on the conquest of Europe in 1939, which had been strictly against the rules since the fall of Napoleon in 1815.

And what of 'Expansionist Russia'? Without much access to the sea for such a gigantic land mass, they managed to fight their way through to the Pacific, opening up the East much as the American pioneers opened up the West. They even managed to annexe Alaska in the interests of fur trapping, and actually worked their way somewhat timidly down the coast of California. Does this explain why the Californian state flag flaunts a bear, with a five pointed red star? Whatever the reason, it is a strange symbol for the home of Rambo and Rocky.

The Russians also ventured to Hawaii. They thought briefly of staying in one of the islands, but soon sickened of bare breasts, grass skirts, and soporific music, and hankered for the familar cold discomfort of Siberia.

Those were the only attempts to expand in the great European tradition. Elsewhere the Russians practised a different method of expansionism. They tended to lean on their neighbours' walls, and when these collapsed under their not inconsiderable weight, they generously helped to rebuild them a little further from home.

Naturally this system had its disadvantages when the time came for colonialism to be a dirty word. They couldn't easily return distant territories to the natives, because they did not possess any. And it is certainly much more difficult and more agonising to break bits off the homeland, like so many squares of a block of chocolate, once association has become a habit. The English experienced this with the two halves of Ireland, the Spaniards with the Basque provinces, and at times with Catalonia, the French with Algeria. If Russia seems expansionist, it is for one reason only – an obsession with defence. Why? Because she has been attacked far more frequently than she has attacked. Admittedly she has occasionally

33

assaulted her immediate neighbours. The Baltic coast was wrested from Sweden; Estonia, Latvia, and Lithuania were absorbed, to say nothing of parts of Poland, and Moldavia. It must be said, however, that when Poland was a powerful kingdom, Moscow was no stranger to its invading army, and at the time of Lithuania's greatness, its territory stretched all the way to the Black Sea.

Russia has only ventured further west than her acquired *cordon sanitaire* when playing her part in a coalition. After the collapse of Nazi Germany, she occupied Berlin to exert her influence on Eastern Europe; and, previously, her troops appeared in Paris as part of the victorious alliance against Napoleon.

But in Europe, from the end of the Middle Ages, when the national ambitions of England, France, Germany and Spain met in fierce antipathy to create, amid much blood, the boundaries of the modern European states, the Russian hardly stepped outside his land. Insularity, homesickness, a lack of security, alien traditions of thought and language, a difficult Cyrillic alphabet made the Russians nervous beyond their borders. When, for a brief period at the end of the Napoleonic Wars, they appeared in Paris, they could not shake off the habits learnt on the steppes of the Kuban. Cossacks, deeply suspicious of city architecture, preferred to bivouac in the wide spaces of the Champs Elysées. They pumped water into their greasy caps and drank. They slaughtered sheep and roasted them on open fires amid the boulevards, for they claimed that 'French food is intolerably bad'.

For the Russian, the homeland is the rock to which he clings. Every step away is a penance, every return is a matter for rejoicing. The fine Italian writer Primo Levi, when he was released from Auschwitz by the Russians, witnessed the Red Army characteristically streaming home, like a mob of large, unruly schoolboys gratefully let out of class. They went in cattle trucks, with beds and wardrobes and curtains, kitted out like village boudoirs. Months of travel lay ahead of them, perhaps as far as Vladivostok or Kamchatka. But they were going home; they were content. Radios squeaked with static, dangerous electric lines made a crazy progress

The Refectory and Church of St. Sergius in the Monastery of St. Sergius at Zagorsk.

The gilded spire – almost 60 metres tall – of the Cathedral of Sts. Peter and Paul, 1715–21, dominates the Leningrad skyline across the River Neva. The Narva triumphal arch, Leningrad, built to commemorate Alexander I's defeat of Napoleon in 1814, is made of granite with a statue of the goddess of Victory in her chariot on top.

from truck to truck. Washing flew bravely from the windows of rumbling carriages. And in the morning, at some tiny wayside halt amid the gorse and sand and pines of the interminable plain, the doors slid back to reveal half-dressed men and women with sleepy peasant faces, who descended with sober dignity to wash in the freezing stream of a water hydrant and then rolled loose tobacco into cigarettes with the pages of *Pravda*.

The uncomfortable truth is that the Russians, far from being the aggressors within Europe, have been invaded time and again by other European powers. Who are we – the inheritors of European power – to tell Russia to forget Napoleon, forget the British and French in the Crimea, forget Hitler? We have wooed them and hated them. In times of crisis, amid catastrophic convulsions of our own making, we cried out for Russian help, against Napoleon, against the Kaiser, against Hitler. And in so many cases theirs was the sacrifice that assured victory, in the snow on the road from Moscow, or among the devastated ruins of Stalingrad. Then with victory achieved (and at what cost!), they became the enemy once more. It is a very curious destiny.

A desire for safety against powers whose enmity and double-dealing has been, in the Russian view, amply proved, explains perhaps that harshness with which Russian influence has been imposed on the peoples of her client states, in Poland, in Czechoslovakia and in Hungary. A story from over there illustrates the point. A Russian and a Polish labourer repairing a derelict house, chance on a horde of gold. The Russian says eagerly, 'We'll share it like brothers.' 'No,' replies the Pole, 'fifty-fifty.'

Huge, suspicious, self-absorbed, part European and part Asian, economically weak or under-developed, an administrative nightmare, wracked by smouldering social forces, Russia came late to the fruits of the European Enlightenment. Her path was strange and tortuous, and the direction she has taken seems hateful to the governments of those countries that we call the 'liberal democracies'.

I note, nonetheless, that Russia anticipated the United States in freedom from slavery, for the serfs were emancipated on the eve of the inauguration of Abraham Lincoln. And I note also, in a land denied the benefits of capitalist technology, that the sputnik went aloft before America sent her manned satellites into the heavens.

This is no land to be looked at with either contempt or fear.

A country so vast that it stretches from the Baltic to the Pacific, from the Arctic Circle to Iran and the Black Sea. A land of some 280 million inhabitants, drawn from an ethnic maze, speaking a myriad local languages. How can such a place be managed?

The solution for government, since Ivan the Terrible, has been to make all power flow from a strong central authority. The trouble with such a rigid system applied to over one sixth of the world's surface is that it cannot possibly know what is going on locally. It cannot conceivably understand or address the problems of communities thousands of miles away. Such unavoidable ignorance in self-important administrators automatically leads to obtuseness and sloth. If this is still true today, how much more true was it in the days before the telegraph and telephone, before the aeroplane and the railway. In fact Russian comic literature is full of incidences of error induced by distance and the resulting negligence. In Gogol's *Dead Souls*, there is corruption in the accountancy of defunct serfs; in the *Inspector General*, there is alarm when a fraudulent official from the capital appears to be conducting an investigation of local civic authorities.

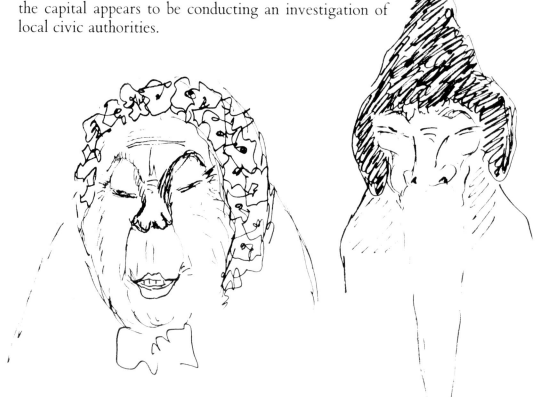

But, against the unitary, centralising impulse of national government, there always existed a strong, conservative, independent pull from the regions. The land was, and is, a huge collection of tribes. That fact is still formally recognised today in the conglomerate that calls itself a Union of Socialist Soviet Republics.

Archeology and historical record indicate that the Russian story began in the south, in the Ukraine. It is said that the first capital of the people who later became 'Russians' was Kiev. Now this is a matter of controversy for many Ukrainians, especially those that live abroad. For although the evidence from the ethnologists and the students of language show that the people of Kiev and the people of Moscow are very closely related, with common roots, the Ukrainians uphold Kiev to be *their* city and nothing to do with those semi-barbarians who inhabit the banks of the River Moskva. When my television series was first shown in Canada, many Ukrainians who live there were upset by my comments about Kiev. Naturally, they thought I should put the expatriate Ukrainian point of view, but I was doing my best to be as objective as possible. I was accused of being a tool of Soviet propaganda, a stigma which should, in fairness, be shared by the Encyclopedia Britannica and other sources above suspicion. It is only too easy to touch a raw nerve and then the old primitive Adam of tribal feeling comes out of the cave, scattering good fellowship to the four winds amid dark mutterings and ugly smears. I recall a row between the delegates at a UNESCO meeting. 'We're not staying here,' huffed some of the Russians, 'we're off to Moscow.' '*You* may be,' replied another Soviet delegate, 'but *I'm* Ukrainian and I'm off to Kiev.'

Never underestimate the strength and importance of regional feeling in the USSR. Almost every Russian, including an outsider like myself, has a Ukrainian ancestor hidden in the upper branches of the family tree. This is so with every other zone in the union. 'I am a Siberian,' says the poet Yevtushenko. So and so is from Lithuania or Estonia; or one is an Uzbek, a Kazakh or a Mongol. That wily old war horse Mikoyan was Armenian. Gromyko, the eternal survivor, now President of the Republic, and a serenely smiling adjunct to

Gorbachev's Russia after over half a century of unrelieved dourness, is from Byelorussia. And Stalin, he of the rich moustache and the inscrutable patriarchal face, was every inch the Georgian. Armenians and Georgians are ancient people, with the long, secret, tenacious memories of tribes that have stood at the crossroads, at the point where Europe flows into Asia. Both peoples, voluntarily joined the Russian confederation in 1802, to gain some protection from the danger of Turkish and Iranian incursions. But the legacy that their long history had bequeathed to the USSR, especially under the Georgian Stalin, is very distinctive and very characteristic, and looks likely to continue under the new Foreign Minister, Shevardnadze.

The peoples in the United States are rather like the drinks in an American bar. The racial bottles are tipped into the cocktail shaker and something gaudy, mixed and surprising is produced. It is a product that places itself, with hand on heart, foursquare under the Stars and Stripes and talks of 'this great country of ours'. That, at least, is the ideal. But in the Russian bar, every bottle is kept separate with its label firmly attached. There are the liquors of the Baltic states, the heavy wines of Georgia, the vodka from Moscow, and whatever fiery potions are brewed in Tashkent, Alma Ata, Irkutsk, or on the Siberian shores of the River Lena.

Many of the challenges and apparent anomalies of the Soviet Union are invariably attributed to the inflexible theories of the Communist Party by those attuned to the very different contradictions of capitalism. In fact, most of these procedural peculiarities are much more the fruit of the Russian imagination than of Marxism.

Let Catherine the Great shed a little light on this as I help her catch her recalcitrant Maltese terrier on the sumptuous lawns of her Summer Palace. The tiny dog, ignoring the tempting plinths of allegorical statues for messages from other canine socialites, gallops over the grass, straight as an arrow, into the distance.

'Russia is a large country,' calls Catherine, 'you won't get out.'

A little later, she begins to share her view of the world.

The Church of the Trinity marks the entrance to the Monastery of the Caves near Kiev. The monastery was founded by monks who inhabited caves in a hill south of Kiev.

'The Italians are wonderful tenors,' she says; 'the French, admirable dancing-masters, the Swiss, unequalled watchmakers, and the Germans, superb kings and queens. And make no mistake about it, that is a trade like any other.'

Naturally, I agree with her, especially since I know that she is German by birth.

She considers that I would make a fine courtier until I draw to her attention the evidence in my possession of gifts to her discarded lovers, all of them fine courtiers too, with a keen sense of what lay beyond the line of duty. This one, 6,000 roubles, and a gift of 500 serfs. The other, less physically reliable, 3,000 thousand roubles and 300 serfs. And so it goes on in a long, reprehensible catalogue.

She eyes me coldly. 'Are you a spy? You must be British.'

Ah yes, prejudice is a two-way traffic.

'Madam,' I say, ignoring her question, 'you must realise that the question is how to reconcile the extraordinarily liberal sentiments you express with the reprehensible autocracy you practise. Despite your gifts of serfs, you have declared that slavery is immoral. Do you deny it?'

'Not for a moment. There is no slavery here, only servitude.'

'Come, come Madam. Is servitude less immoral than slavery?'

'No. My desire is to put an end to it. But I have not the power as yet to enforce my desire. The investment in the past is too great. Anyone must be careful when trying to swim against the tide of Russian history. And then, what will the serfs do with their freedom? They have had absolutely no training in its exploitation. They will feel lost without orders, and resentful, like my terrier. Wouldn't you?' she spoke to it directly. It responded with the feeble wag of its little tail.

'Even the highest ideals, when put into practice, become pragmatic,' she declared. 'A ship proceeds in a general direction, never in a straight line. It is buffeted by winds and waves, and obeys the forces of nature for a little while, but it never loses track of the general direction. Finally, it arrives in port despite the little traps nature sets for it.'

*Worshippers arrive at Vladimir Cathedral for the service on Reed (Palm) Sunday (top right).
The old, never far from the churches, hold their own council (top left). The Metropolitan
arrives to conduct the well-attended service (above).*

Two world wars and the October Revolution seem to have had little effect on this ancient
citizen as she watches the world from the steps of Kiev Cathedral.

'There is another possible fate for a ship,' I ventured.

'And what is that?' she asked, her eyes narrowing.

'It can sink.'

She laughed.

'You amuse me. It's a pity you are not 20 years younger. And I 10 years older.'

Concealing my irritation, I make another effort to call the terrier.

'Don't bother,' she said. 'When I leave, he will follow me without being called. He is a dog, you see, not a bitch.'

The Soviet government has been unable to shake off its Russian past, and by the same token, one feels that Catherine would have understood and even applauded some of the initiatives taken today. She would have been perfectly capable of engaging Mr Gorbachev in a dialectical argument about measures to be taken in an ideal world, while being very cautious about giving her consent to the practical application of such measures. It was perhaps because of this dichotomy between the odious practical necessity and the lofty, theoretical pipe-dream, that so many of her intimates went by the name of philosopher. To satisfy the other side of her nature, her lovers were everything from libertine princes to randy sergeants.

The traveller in such a vast, varied land may well find reason to be momentarily grateful for the grip of authority and discipline. When we filmed in Moscow, we were allowed to record and photograph whatever rehearsals or performances we wished. We filmed a whole act of *Boris Godunov* at the Bolshoi without a murmur of complaint, despite the fact that we blew a series of fuses by plugging into a 127 volt circuit! We had authority, and that was that. Now, I cannot imagine what troubles we would have had in the West. What difficulties, what arguments, what calculations! What extra payments, what featherbeds, what demarcation disputes! I make no judgment as to the rights and wrongs of union contracts in the West, but I sighed with relief at the ease of our progress in Moscow.

The State is the nanny, for good or bad, and keeps a stern eye on the conduct of the children. And this is said to be, as in the best

regulated English households, for the good of the little dears. Once, when we were photographing an international women's basketball match, I observed the medical auxiliaries seated by the court. They looked as forbidding as rock faces, and so very Victorian. Their dress was halfway between that of the surgeon and that of the butcher, and you knew perfectly well that they were a grim warning to the players not to get hurt. Just like dear old nanny.

The sudden rush of Soviet emigrés returning home from the USA need surprise nobody. If the choice is between opportunity and security, the sight of an American income tax form, with its convoluted phrases and indiscreet questions, all couched in a language which hovers on the borders of comprehensibility even for a native, may well be the deciding factor.

Outside the children's theatre in Novosibirsk, the young audience makes its way past a musical fountain.

There is a limit, however, to state control. It seemed to me that the Soviet government was well aware of the shaky base on which their central authority has been built. Their television, for example, which one might expect to be a good, state-controlled conduit for propaganda, for the mind-control of the masses, was, I found, rather bland. It was, if anything, doggedly informative, with an earnest desire to explain. There was no subtle, psychological persuasion, none of the distortions and tricks that our Western television so exuberantly devotes to the selling of cornflakes, dog food and political parties. The Russian commentator is no mighty pundit, no small screen superman like Walter Cronkite or Robin Day; he is rather a mild professorial gent, seated against a background of library books, who gives a long and judicious report of whatever is going on from the Soviet point of view. The most abrasive remark I heard throughout the whole of my Russian journey was, 'Meanwhile in Cairo, the vaudeville continues.' That, considering the maelstrom in the Middle East, is mild indeed. It is as though there were a need even to defuse non-existent situations, to render the news bland and unabrasive. Mrs Thatcher once told me, with all the weight of her authority, that there was no public opinion in Russia. I remember my reply: 'I suppose, Prime Minister, that is why the Russians have had two major revolutions this century, while the British have only had football riots and a few bitter strikes.'

The truth is that the Soviet Communist Party today is as respectful of public opinion as any party in British politics. It is compelled to be.

In the words of my great-uncle, Alexander Benois, both founder of the magazine. '*Mir Iskusstva*' (The World of Art), and a pillar of the Russian Ballet, the Russian attitude towards the arts is one of piety. Certainly if a reputable poet begins declaiming his work in public, traffic is diverted, the poet is not interrupted, the crowd is not dispersed. The reverence towards talent is such that the artist occupies a much more important role in Soviet society than in any country in that the part of the world which calls itself free. It may even be said that so important is the place reserved for the artist, that

Tolstoy's snow-covered house at Yasnaya Polyana (Clear Glade). He lived here after he married Sophia Andreevna Bers in 1862, until he died in 1910. The house has been kept exactly as it was when Sophia died in 1919. Tolstoy was buried in the middle of the old wood, not far from the house, with no stone or plaque to mark his grave at his own request.

The actor Lev Durov, made up as Tolstoy for the television series, sitting at Tolstoy's desk at Yasnaya Polyana.

he or she even merit persecution should they be using the influence accorded them to discredit or denounce the dictates of central authority.

There is an inherent irony in this. It suggests a form of spirituality, even a belief not that distant from religion. To read, re-read, learn by heart, and cherish the works of Dostoyevsky, Tolstoy, Chekhov, Pushkin; to open the sensibilities to the abstract persuasion of Tchaikovsky, Mussorgsky, Borodin, Prokofiev; to stand in rapt attention before the masters of the visual arts; all these activities are, in a very real sense, a form of belief. One remembers Lenin's reflection on hearing Beethoven's Appassionata Sonata, which he had played for him on every possible occasion – 'Of what is man *not* capable?'

In our section of the world, classics are read less frequently or thoroughly, and the theatre and opera are supposed to pay for themselves as far as possible. The arts are considered superficial decorations on the structure of life, not a vital part of the structure itself.

One of my interviews in the television programme is with Tolstoy. He is played by the excellent actor Lev Durov, who was made up and wigged in Moscow, and transported by limousine to Yasnaya Polyana, Tolstoy's house. About 40 kilometres away from its destination, the car was stopped by a Soviet highway patrol, probably eager to know what an official limousine was doing so far from the capital, thundering along at such a pace on the black ice in midwinter.

Looking into the interior, the Soviet highway cop practically had a heart attack, for among the cushions at the back sat Tolstoy – oblivious to the outside world, rehearsing his lines – appearing to talk to himself, a typical pastime in extreme old age.

After an explanation, the car was allowed to continue. When we had completed the scene, we sent Mr Durov back in another car, while we continued to shoot the interior of the house for an hour or two. Then we all piled into the limousine, and set off speedily along the same route to Moscow.

On the way, 40 kilometres away from the house, we were stopped by a road-block. Many patrolmen, including some off duty in civilian clothes, were all eager to see Tolstoy. They were bitterly disappointed to discover that the limousine held nothing but a television crew and that he had escaped their net in a smaller car.

Can you imagine an American patrolman recognising Mark Twain in a chauffeur-driven vehicle, or an English bobby feeling himself in the presence of Dickens? Add to this the fact that Tolstoy's house was saved from destruction by workers from a local factory during the last war. They attacked the Nazi cohorts prematurely and doggedly held on to the building until the arrival of the advancing Red Army. Prior to that, during the great retreat before Hitler's relentless advance, all the contents of the historic house were evacuated to Siberia in a specially heated train, at a time when every other train was pressed into service for the evacuation of armies and the transport of munitions to the front. This is an example of Soviet priorities.

I remember my drama school in London as a preparation for an idealised theatre, a theatre which does not exist, a kind of altruistic temple of the arts. Emerging into the theatre as it is, and adapting its realities, entailed a degree of disillusion, a lowering of the sights, and an acceptance of what is known as show-biz, with all its razzamatazz, glitz and tinsel.

Such a transition is not called for in the Soviet Union. In a sense, most of the actors are eternal students of drama, going straight from school to fixed companies which are constituted along the same lines as the schools, never indulging in long runs, nor subject to strictly commercial considerations. They play two or three times a week, and they are never unduly taxed by dreary routine. They also maintain that juvenile integrity, that sense of artistic virginity, which we are encouraged to lose as quickly as possible, in order to make life liveable.

The Mossoviet Theatre in Moscow has had a play of mine, *Halfway Up The Tree*, in its repertory for over 10 years. Its leading

I joined a group of twelve actors from the Mossoviet Theatre, Moscow, after a matinée performance of my play Halfway Up The Tree *which had just completed its tenth year in the repertory.*

actor, Rostislav Plyat, gathered the actors together in the green room when I first went to see it.

The cast sat there with their pads and pencils at the ready.

'How can we make the play more English?' inquired Plyat.

'It is already almost painfully English,' I replied, 'a most penetrating and uncomfortable picture of the delights of a certain English village life. You do it marvellously.'

There was no recognition of this accolade.

'Mr Ustinov,' said Mr Plyat sternly, 'we are not here to flatter each other. Our approval of you is expressed in our performance of your play. Your approval of us is expressed in your kind words. Now that that is out of the way, let me ask you again – how can we make the play more English?'

I appealed to logic.

'What is the point of making it even more English?' I asked. 'Few of your public will ever go there, fewer still have been there.'

'It is our business to impose a sense of Englishness on them,' he flashed. 'Whether they have been there or not, whether they ever go there or not, it is our duty as artists to make them realise up to what a point your play is English!' He changed his tune to one of soberness, tempered with steel.

'I will now ask you for a third time. How can we make the play more English?'

Clearly I would have to find a way. I hesitated. At length I said, 'Well, perhaps ... '

All the pads and pencils came up into the ready position. I was clearly cracking.

'Perhaps,' I went on, 'the cross on the vicar's bible is a little on the large side, in the light of the fact that the religion is Anglican and not Catholic.'

They all wrote furiously.

'Why did you not say so at once?' asked the great actor.

Not all contacts are quite as serious.

Professor Arnold Katz, the excellent conductor of the superb Philharmonic Orchestra of Novosibirsk, in Siberia, listened to my

I was amused to find a poster in Moscow advertising Spartacus, a film I made 30 years ago.
It appears to be a big hit in Moscow today!

At Zagorsk, the seat of orthodoxy, young monks are still put through their paces by their older brothers, as they were in centuries past.

request for the possibility of shooting the rehearsal. 'Certainly,' he replied, 'but do you want them to play well, as they do at a concert, or should they play badly, and I give them hell?'

It was almost a relief for our jaded spirits to find a trace of innocent larceny in this exhausting atmosphere of artistic truth.

Artistic truth, as we have seen, is a variation on religious truth. Religion, in the strict Marxist view, is still the opium of the people and therefore frowned upon. On the other hand, the traditions of the Orthodox faith have a strong hold on the imagination of the people, and so public worship (for the Orthodox and others) is grudgingly permitted, within certain guidelines. A church, depending on the mysterious operation of authority, may be a place devoted to the service of God, or a museum to superstition.

The latter, which is fairly common, may seem blasphemous and ugly. But this was not the impression I got when I entered a couple of these ex-churches. These are not places besmirched by crude atheist propaganda. The Russians intend them to be, with sincerity and perhaps even reverence, Temples to Reason. They are yet another example of the trait I noticed on Soviet television, the desire to educate, to explain, to reason. These museums are designed to show how religion was deliberately used by the old ruling classes to subdue, cheat and dominate the working proletariate. Religion was, to continue in the language of Marxism, a weapon in the class war. Now this, even to believers, is an interesting and almost acceptable point of view. And the attempt to replace the concept of Divinity with a concept of Reason is a perfectly sober and respectable undertaking, not very different from, and certainly no more outrageous than, the intention of our famous philosopher Bertrand Russell when he wrote *Why I am Not a Christian*.

The greatest complaint against these Temples of Reason is not that they show a violent, unprincipled atheism, but that they are rather dull. The services of the Russian Orthodox Rite, on the other hand, are anything but dull. In mystery and colour, tradition and beauty they provide all that the museums lack. In an odd way, Soviet authority has catered for all tastes: for reasonable doubt, and for irrational faith.

Paradox lies at the core of so much Russian behaviour. To try to enter the heart of it, I summon up the memory of Fedor Mikhailovich Dostoyevsky, the great prophet of paradox. What a life! Fedor the epileptic, the depressive, the manic labourer in the workhouse of poverty and the imagination. His miserable father was murdered by his own serfs, yet Fedor was the champion of the serfs. In 1849, as a member of a revolutionary circle, he was condemned to death and led out to the place of execution. At the very last minute a horseman galloped up with a pardon, which banished him to prison and privation in Siberia. Dare I question this sufferer, this victim, this giant? What would he say to me?

'Fedor Mikhailovich – you made a wonderful speech to the memory of Pushkin. It was of evident sincerity and colossal power. You said that Russia's destiny was to revitalise the world by the example of its selflessness and brotherly love.'

'What is sincere one moment,' he cautions me, 'is suspect the next. The mood of an occasion can drive perfectly rational people into the wildest enthusiasm which they may reject in the next instant. But at least at this moment, at the moment of my reply, I see that Russians are the only people who can perceive that suffering is the only path to the possibility of future happiness. Everything is purified by suffering. Every moment of felicity must be paid for in the coin of misery.'

'And is that so in your case, when you faced the moment of execution, when you suffered in Siberian exile and as a Private in the Army? What compensation did you receive? Don't you resent those wasted and tragic years?'

'Wasted and tragic? No! My suffering gave me everything: my literature, my characters, my understanding, my compassion. Why should I resent a superficial injustice? I am grateful, even thankful, to the fools, the idiots who sentenced me to be shot.'

From one of the lowest circles in hell, I see the ranks of the despots, the spies, the informers, the secret police arise and cry out

In Dostoevsky's room where everything has remained as it was when he died. A half-finished manuscript and a note from his daughter lie on the desk; the candles are lit every day and a glass of fresh tea is left for him.

in justification: 'Why do you blame us for what was done to Fedor Mikhailovich? Are we not in part responsible for some of the greatest books in the history of man?'

That is a very Russian response.

'I see you are packing,' I say. 'Are you leaving?'

'We are going to Western Europe tomorrow,' he replies.

'The West!' I exclaim. 'You like it there?'

'I hate it,' he murmurs, 'but what other way is there to rediscover Russia than by going abroad?'

In Tolstoy's house, the pretty young guide was explaining to us just how inconsiderate the great man's wife could be.

'But,' I protested, 'don't you think he must have been intolerable to live with?'

'Oh, I do so agree with you.' And that pretty young person looked at me with great relief.

The differences between life in the West and life in the Soviet Union are, for obvious reasons, exaggerated by newspapers and other forces of the media. But the observer who travels extensively will be struck, by the similarities everywhere in human nature itself, which easily transcends the superficial influence of politics.

Once, some years ago, on a freezing winter day in Leningrad, I was watching on Soviet television a football match between the USSR and Sweden being played in the southern city of Tbilisi, in Georgia. The game was undistinguished, but the weather in the south was fine and warm. The grass was green and the trees were in leaf, and the spectators were relaxing in their shirt-sleeves. It was pleasant to look at from a city which was buried under a blanket of ice and snow.

At the end of the first half, one of those sad, stately women who abound in the Soviet Union appeared on the screen, the bun at the back of her head making her look like a ballet-mistress of discreet refinement. She informed us that our treat for half-time was a visit to the Supreme Soviet, to hear a selection of the morning's speeches.

The magnificent Church of Our Lady of Kazan, 1671 (top) stands in the old estate of the Tsars near Kolomenskoe where Peter the Great took refuge from the revolt of the Streltsy. The Church of the Ascension, 1532 (above) was commissioned by Vasili III in thanks for the birth of his son, who became Ivan the Terrible.

The golden domes of orthodoxy gleam against the bright winter sky.

Brezhnev huddled with Kosygin in the background, while in the foreground another delegate was addressing an absolutely immobile audience. 'I don't understand the language,' said my wife, 'but I seem to recognise the speech.' Then suddenly, in mid-sentence, the screen went blank and I thought, 'What's this? A power cut?' Not at all. The melancholy lady with the bun was back to announce the start of the second half of the football match.

Later, I spoke of this to our hall porter, a tough-looking joe who stood no nonsense. He gave me a bleak look. 'Listen,' he said, 'if we'd lost one single second of that football match to hear any more of that political crap, there would have been another revolution in Russia.'

Sport has become a great source of confidence in the Soviet Union, and the free exchange of athletes is a civilising force in this nuclear world. It is one method of learning about each other, among many others, and let's face it, we all have much more to learn from each other than we have to teach each other.

On Lithuanian television, I saw Boris Becker win his first Wimbledon, and, but for some details of the Russian commentary, I might have been sitting in Geneva or Los Angeles. The commentator, a Russian lady who had played at Wimbledon, was impressed by the tennis. But she thought Becker was a shade young for such an honour. That comment, I thought, was characteristic. In the view of certain elderly Russians, Brezhnev could have won Wimbledon if only he had put his mind to it.

The bugbear of the Russians is the character of Oblomov, a superb creation of the novelist Goncharov. He is a man of such inspired sloth, that his indolence is lifted into the stratosphere of poetry. He is as redolent of a certain Russia as Don Quixote is a symbol of the Spanish capacity for self-delusion, or the good soldier Schweik is the epitome of the Czech art of survival, or Falstaff the hot-air balloon of English bluster and benevolence.

If today a Russian policeman is encouraged to give out tickets for dirty cars, it is the most recent phase in the endless battle against the Oblomov in their midst.

We met Oblomov, waking Rip Van Winkle-like from a siesta of 130 years.

'How did you get in here?' he asks in alarm.

'Well, the door was open and I just walked in.'

'Where's that servant? Did I send him to town? I can't remember. That's just like servants, isn't it? The moment you want them, they're gone. And you have to have them, simply because everyone else has them. There's no other reason.'

'You seem rather out of sorts.'

'Yes, yes. I'm exhausted. But for that I could have done so many interesting and wonderful things in life. By the way, why didn't the dog bark when you entered?'

'I don't know. I passed it but it was asleep.'

'So that's how it is. I read somewhere that animals and masters become more and more alike as time goes on.'

'Wouldn't you be better off if you married?'

'I have thought about it, and yet ... you know even the most insignificant women, those entirely devoid of character, have an awful habit of acquiring personality if you marry them, and it is they who make marriage so perilous.'

'Oblomov, think!'

'No, no.' And he hid his head briefly under the bedclothes. 'It's the last thing I must do,' he whispered when he emerged cautiously. 'It could be fatal. The doctor tells me that a man in my fragile condition should not be made to think.'

'Perhaps I'd better go?'

'Yes, do. Because I can't find my servant. He's probably in town. I think I'll profit from his absence by taking 40 winks. Would you mind going out the back way?'

'Why?'

'If you leave by the front the dog might bark and that would wake me up.'

Russia strikes you as a land of strictly applied rules. But sometimes this rigidity is shaken when one set of apparently sacrosanct rules is replaced by another, as inflexible. I remember asking the aged Tolstoy – 'Is it true that a few years ago, in your early eighties, you declared sexual intercourse immoral?'

Tolstoy searched dimly among his memories, then nodded his assent.

'You didn't always think that,' I suggested.

He thought for a moment, flushed with anger, and brought his fist down hard on his desk.

'It is what I think *now* which is important!' he roared.

CHAPTER THREE

A SENSE OF WHAT WAS

A Soviet wedding is more like a church wedding than a civil one. The dispensing authority in the Palace of Wedlock in Kiev is a woman dressed like a druid. Lenin hangs on the wall, far larger than life, and in a minstrel's gallery sits an orchestra with folk instruments, playing hymeneal ditties on cue during gaps in the ritual. The relatives seem as moved by the situation as they would be in one of our chapels, and after all the admonitions and solemnities, the National Anthem reminds them of their duties as a young Soviet couple.

Before riding off in the traditional white limousine, with the intertwined wedding rings on the roof, much like the Olympic symbol, they kiss their families goodbye, clutching the flowers they have been given. On the way to the airport or railway station, at the beginning of their honeymoon, the vehicle stops at the tombs of warriors, known or unknown. The young couple bend to place the flowers before the resting place of their choice, and then stand for a minute or two, hand in hand, thinking of those deprived of the joys of youth by their sacrifice. This is tradition. It is expected, and it is decent. Had almost half of the United States been occupied by an invader, and had it required the sacrifice of 20 million lives to free the country of this blight, the same kind of habit would doubtless have taken root over there.

Outside Leningrad and at Babi-Yar in Kiev, there are perhaps the most harrowing of these graveyards. In Volgograd, virtually a new city, there is some evidence of that ferocious orgy of destruction remembered by the name of Stalingrad. It is quite usual to see undulations in the ground, each covering the remains of thousands of bodies. The same is true of what is left of the notorious concentration camp of Bergen-Belsen, where the deaths were too numerous and too indiscriminate for there to be any identification other than a date, usually merely a year, inscribed on a single plaque. Every Sunday, the graveyards are full. Many of the visitors clearly come regularly; those with missing limbs, those who limp or walk with the help of crutches, those who are merely lonely, and seek company. Here an old woman weeps silently, a handkerchief pushed into her face by thick, twisted fingers, while there a veteran in a wheel-chair looks facts in the face, unflinchingly, without emotion. In the centre of this concentrated act of remembrance, the heat from the eternal flame makes the scene reverberate, as though the stillness had a massive pulse.

The Russian people see no glamour in war. It would be too much to expect. They are willing to leave the Rockys and the Rambos and the Amerikas, together with other fruits of fevered imagination to those who have been largely spared the sickening realities of occupation and conflict. Since the beginning of recorded history, foreign armies have crossed the frontiers of Russia, and the frontiers themselves have shifted with each exhausting test of strength. First of all they came from the east, the grinning soldiers of fortune, as cruel as they were dispassionate. They boasted terrifying names, the Tartars, the Pechenegs, the Polovtsians, the Golden Horde. They destroyed all that stood in their way, and eventually exacted ruinous taxes from the humiliated Russians.

The inhabitants of the Ukraine were separated from the other Russians, pushed westward. Their language became impregnated with Polish words. Kiev was razed to the ground, and the capital became Moscow, after tough competition from the other towns of

the so-called Golden Ring around Moscow – Rostov, Vladimir, Yaroslavl, Suzdal, and the proud city-state of Novgorod, safe from the Mongol terror because of its geographic position, but right in the path of that greater Nazi terror some seven centuries later.

If it was not the Mongols, it was the Teutonic Knights, the Lithuanians, the Swedes, or the Poles, who occupied territories around Moscow. Then it was the Turks, always eager to prevent a Russian breakthrough to the Black Sea. It was during these interminable conflicts that the Russian army was forged into an effective fighting force from disorganised levies. The first naval victory over the Turks, as well as military success against both the Swedes and the Turks, made Europe aware that here was a force to be reckoned with, and Western nervousness became a reality.

From then on, Russia was solicited as an ally, and began to contribute to the events of the day, such as the partitions of Poland with the Prussians and Austrians. She continued to struggle against the Turks, and participated in the alliances against Napoleon, culminating in the French invasion, the occupation and burning of Moscow, the scorched earth policy, and the eventual entry of allied troops into Paris.

On the road from Vilnyus in Lithuania to the Baltic Sea, stands an oak tree, known as Napoleon's Oak, under which he is supposed to have pitched his tent on his way to conquer Russia.

In 1807, Napoleon and Alexander I met on a barge at Tilsit on the River Nieman. It was a symbolic meeting arranged by the French and Russian chiefs of protocol. Alexander, naive and idealistic, was overwhelmed by Napoleon who was on his best behaviour, putting to good use his suave Gallic charm. The meeting resulted in a highly-charged treaty of friendship.

However, in 1812 Napoleon invaded Russia. It started well for the French, with the Russians beating retreat under the command of General Barclay de Tolly. At the battle of Borodino the Russians held their ground, but it was an inconclusive battle despite all Napoleon's military skills. The scorched earth policy was created, and towns, houses, fields and forests were burned; Moscow was

Rostov is one of the cities which make up the Golden Ring around Moscow. The Kremlin walls proved more decorative than successful as a defence. Two ceremonial gateways were built into the walls, each with a church and two towers. The Gate Church of St. John the Evangelist (above) was built in 1683.

abandoned so that when Napoleon made a victorious entry, the empty streets rang with the sound of French horses' hooves.

Napoleon could neither advance into Russia, nor stay where he was with winter coming, nor go back and admit defeat. His attempts to remind Alexander of their previous friendship – 'remember the good times we had on the raft at Tilsit' – were rejected and the inevitable French retreat began. Marshal Kutusov drove Napoleon from Russia along the same route that he had invaded in order to rub his nose in the destruction he had caused.

Alexander was obsessed with the idea of being a peacemaker, and to this end he drew up an extraordinary document which reflected his belief that nations could settle their differences according to a set of rules. He believed that a European Confederation would be possible, even a League of Nations! He was, indeed, a visionary.

Only about 40 years later came the squalid farce of the Crimean War, a campaign without a cause. It resulted from an ultimatum delivered by the British, French, and Turkish governments, which threatened the Russians with war unless certain conditions were fulfilled. The requisite conditions were indeed fulfilled, but since typhus had broken out in Varna, the Bulgarian town which was the Allied Headquarters, it was deemed wiser to launch an invasion rather than send soldiers home in quarantine. The campaign was a textbook illustration of the irresponsibility, cruelty and waste of war. The British admiralty possessed a map of the area, but the depth of the water near the Perekop peninsula, connecting Crimea to the mainland, was not marked. Consequently, the British warships ran aground. The French did not even possess a map. They had to rely on two water-colours painted by the unsuspecting French artist Raffet. The paintings were impounded as vital military documents and the poor painter was grilled for extra information. 'Try to recall that bit over there. Is that a road? Where does it lead? Describe the terrain to the left of your picture.'

The French also used, for the first time in history, a form of telegraph linking the Emperor to his field commanders. This enabled Napoleon III to instruct his generals where to attack on the basis of

The Cathedral of the Dormition, Rostov (above) is just visible over the Kremlin wall. It faces the Gate and Church of the Resurrection, 1670. The top picture shows the domes of the Gate Church of St. John the Evangelist, Rostov.

the two water-colours. The French general, Pelissier, resigned his command with the ominous remark, 'War is becoming increasingly impossible at the paralysing end of an electric cable.'

The Russian officers were no more competent than their opponents. Lord Lucan, at the height of the charge of the Light Brigade, reined in his horse to ask a Russian artillery officer about the health of a society hostess in Paris who had once entertained both men. Lord Raglan, a general of the old school who had been Wellington's secretary at Waterloo in 1815, habitually referred to his French allies as 'the enemy.'

'Tomorrow, at dawn, we attack the French.'

'But sir ...'

'What, do you dare to contradict me? When I was a puppy of your age I knew how to remain silent.'

And at dawn:

'My lord, the French emissaries have arrived.'

'Ha, very good. So they have the sense to surrender?'

'Not quite, my lord.'

'What else can they do? We have 'em outnumbered, do we not? Ah monsieur, there you are. Well?'

'I must protest, my lord. By some mistake your cannons are facing towards us.'

'As indeed they should be.'

'No, no. We are your allies.'

'What allies? Is this true? Why was I not reminded?'

'But sir, I tried to ...'

'Damn you, sir, with your perpetual interruptions. Will you not be quiet?'

For us, the story of Florence Nightingale's noble humanitarian effort and the honest reporting of William Russell in *The Times* have made the Crimean campaign a metaphor for military stupidity.

The Great War of 1914 began with very much the same stultifying attitudes as the Crimean War, but it is now remembered for the gigantic scale of operations, as though a simple whistled tune had

The Convent of the Intercession, 1364, Suzdal (top). It was once used as a women's prison for any troublesome members of the royal household and noble families. Today, parts of the convent are being restored as a hotel, restaurant and concert hall. Above is the Church of Sts. Boris and Gleb at Kideksha, near Suzdal, 1152.

The museum of wooden architecture at Suzdal (top). The Refectory Church of the Dormition (above left) in the Monastery of the Saviour and St. Euthymius, Suzdal built in 1525. The dark domes of the Cathedral of the Nativity of the Virgin (above right) rise above the town of Suzdal. The church was built in 1225.

At the museum of wooden architecture at Suzdal, many of Russia's wooden churches are reassembled to preserve them. However, many can still be found in a dilapidated state in remote parts of the countryside. The Church of the Transfiguration, 1756 (above) was brought to the museum from the village of Kozlyatyevo.

The Cathedral of St. Dmitry, at Vladimir, 1194–7. This magnificent church is beautifully decorated with stone carvings, which include plants, griffins, peacocks and lions.

been orchestrated to symphonic proportions, and the conductors, many of them, had lost all control over the instruments. Russia, by her precipitate mobilisation and rash offensive, saved the war from being lost, even if she was no longer there at the moment of victory. She was in the grip of revolution, facing a resurgent Poland, and with a German occupation of the Ukraine. Then came an event conveniently overlooked today, the invasion of the Soviet Union by British, French, Canadian, American and Japanese troops, attempting to nip the Communist experiment in the bud. It is overlooked perhaps because it was unsuccessful, which is precisely why it is remembered by every Soviet schoolchild, as the earliest battle honours of the Red Army after the revolution itself.

Hitler's invasion of 1941 was by far the most costly in life and destruction in this recurrent pattern of events. The Russians have absolutely no desire whatever to renew the experience with all the improved lethal possibilities of today. They realise that the next escalation will be the last. They are attached to life. Their respect for the dead is a measure of this attachment. And yet there are those who regard Russia as expansionist, and as the enemy. Why? Because there are those the world over, in America, in Europe, yes and in Russia, who find it difficult to live without an enemy. The idea of an enemy is reassuring, it reinforces mental laziness. You know where you stand without having to reassess your position all the time.

And then let's face it, in a market-oriented society, an enemy is good for business. That is perhaps the greatest stumbling-block for those who admit that whoever uses the nuclear weapon first will be a war criminal on a scale which makes the wretches of Nuremberg look like juvenile delinquents. For the time being, possession of a so-called nuclear deterrent is regarded as a practical advantage instead of being morally reprehensible. Until such attitudes change, there will always be enemies around to satisfy the simple-minded, and to tell fools where their duty lies.

The past lives. Every aspect of it is lovingly tended and used to illuminate the present. At the Geological Institute in Siberia, a

The blackened remains of a Siberian man and his horse, preserved for nearly 4,000 years in the frozen ground, now lie in the Hermitage, Leningrad.

mammoth has been dug up from the oblivion of the bog and the permafrost. It is a baby mammoth, its stomach still full of undigested grass. In the basement of the Hermitage, in Leningrad, I saw the remains of a man, a proto-Russian, frozen into permanence perhaps some 2,000 years before Christ. It is a most extraordinary sight. The body is perfectly recognisable but it is dark and wizened and has the texture of rubber, like those black pieces of tyre thrown to the side of the road by trucks. The features of the body are quite clear, almost solid, not at all like the thin, delicate and dessicated features of the Egyptian mummies.

This Siberian body still has eyelashes. The toenails and fingernails are grotesquely long. The teeth are intact, standing out from the gums which have shrunk away. It is astonishing. In the interests of decency his loins are covered with a kind of hessian cloth. His wife also exists but she is not displayed. It is said that the metal ornaments which she wore around her wrists and ankles, corroded into the body so that her extremities fell off when she was discovered and exposed to the air. A horse and chariot were also rescued from this same burial site. The chariot wheels are enormous, the hub stands nearly as tall as my shoulder, and between the wheels there is a little basket-like platform with a sort of sun-fringe on top. The horse lies almost in a foetal position, as if it had shrunk into itself like a dead fly.

Who was this man? He was obviously a man of northern climates, for the gigantic wheels of the chariot are well-adapted for the snows. He had reddish or carrot-coloured hair and he was beginning to go grey. From the length of his bones it appears that he was perhaps six foot tall, astonishingly tall for such an ancient specimen. Old maps show Russia to have been empty. The old maps were wrong.

'The road ahead,' Lenin said, surprising as it may seem to some, 'lies in the contemplation of the past. We have arrived here only through experience of what has gone before. We will change but we will not forget. The evidence that leads us to revolution is taken from a profound understanding of history and its success must be based on the conviction of our humanity.'

When we were filming in Lithuania we came across a whole village carefully reconstructed in the old style of wooden architecture. Some of the buildings were original. They had been gathered from distant places, dismantled and re-assembled on this site. Others were very exact reproductions, faithful down to the last detail. Everything was simple, yet very beautiful. A family did the caretaking, an elderly couple whose uneventful lives made it appear all the more as if they were embedded in 18th-century Lithuania.

The old woman had a sister who lived in Canada, where there are many Lithuanian communities. When she discovered that we were a Canadian film crew she broke down and wept. Messages were pressed on us and photographs were taken of family poses and exchanged. Thousands of questions were answered as best we could, healths were drunk. They wept and then we wept. It was a touching moment. Once again, here was the evidence that humanity is the strongest of all links.

In the marshland outside Novgorod some bills from the past have been discovered, scratched on tree bark. They are the notices of barbers and tradesmen from many centuries ago: a beard trim, a haircut, or a pomade for so many rubles. Bits of old instruments have been reconstituted and the techniques for playing them rediscovered. Sometimes the ordinary is more eloquent than the extraordinary.

At moments I have thought that to the Russian the past is more real than the present. I once suggested that Mrs Thatcher's nostalgia for Victorian values would be largely satisfied in the Soviet Union. It is a very conservative nation.

When a Russian writer dies, his house or his study immediately becomes a shrine. Old ladies, as tough as battle-axes, look after the holy place and its memories. From wobbly wicker chairs with well-dented seats, the ancient vestal virgins eye the visitor with unblinking stares. Watch that glass case, it's not there for the idle to lean upon! Do not breathe on that frame, the moisture will tarnish the gilt! The very definition of vigilance.

Vilnyus (top and above left), the capital of Lithuania. Lithuania is one of the three Baltic republics, together with Latvia and Estonia. All three were independent between the two world wars but are now republics within the Soviet Federation. Vilnyus stands where the rivers Neris and Vilen meet, and was badly damaged during the last war when it was occupied by the Germans. Trakay Castle (above right) lies 28 kilometres west of Vilnyus. Built of brick in the 15th century, it stands in isolation on an island.

After we had filmed the Hermitage, I remember that a speech was required of me. I told our hosts that if only the old ladies had been there at the time of the Bolshevik Revolution, the storming of the Winter Palace in Leningrad might never have happened. The revolutionaries would have been forced to line up at the cloakroom exchanging their machine-guns for numbered tickets. These old ladies are indomitable and intrepid. I sometimes think that the Russian victory over Hitler was due in part to this formidable regiment of women.

But this severity is only the mask worn by reverence and affection. When we visited Dostoyevsky's room I saw that there was even a little note on his desk saying, 'Daddy, I love you. Signed, Lyuba,' left where Lyuba had put it. The clock on the mantel was stopped at the minute of his death. Nothing had been disturbed. As we entered I said to the old ladies, 'Please don't come in while we are working, it's distracting and we'll have to begin again.' But when I was halfway through my text the door creaked open slowly and in came one of the ladies with a glass of tea, not for me, but for Dostoyevsky. She placed the hot, steaming glass on the desk and took away the glass from yesterday, cold and covered with a thin sprinkling of dust. Her manner was discreet but defiant, and when she went out I thought I detected a look of abstract triumph on her face.

That is the kind of trouble you are liable to run into when you intrude into Russian history.

And in the little southern town of Taganrog, on the Sea of Azov, there was another stern guardian spirit awaiting us in the doorway of Chekhov's house. She held in her hand a long pointer made of glass, a weapon that she brandished like Don Quixote confronting the windmill. The house was small and the rooms were pokey. The old lady was frail and her sight was none too good, so it required considerable agility to keep out of the way of her waving glass wand.

That was not the only memorial to Chekhov in the little town. Part of the school that Chekhov attended was given over to a permanent exhibition. There, in a glass case, was his suit, his hat, his

Chekhov's hat, coat, bow tie and walking stick are kept behind glass at his school in Taganrog.

bow tie, his walking stick. It was as if all these things were ready for him to walk out of the door at any minute. There was a theatre in the town, too, the oldest and largest theatre in southern Russia. In this theatre, in continuous repertory, they perform either Chekhov's plays or dramatisations of his short stories. The place had a soft glow to it and I told our hosts that it was warm in Chekhov's shadow.

Taganrog is Chekhov's shrine. But it is something more than a mere memorial, dead and cold. The whole town is a living celebration of a great artist and, perhaps more importantly, a constant encouragement to his art. There is the Chekhov family grocery shop, stocked with the teas, sugar and flour of everyday business, and the little luxuries imported from Paris or London that the gentry of Chekhov's young days valued so highly. And there are the jottings, in Anton's own hand, in the account book, evidence that his father's frequent absence forced the youthful playwright to mind the shop. In the drawing-room upstairs, Chekhov first tried his hand as a dramatist. Today, a little company performs in that shop twice a week, and it becomes so crowded in the narrow space that sometimes the actors even outnumber the audience.

I watched them play an adaptation of a Chekhov short story. It was the story of a woman who takes refuge in an inn from her husband who is pursuing her, and it tells of all the things that happen to her before her husband arrives. There were perhaps eight in the audience and twelve actors. They acted with such intimacy, as if we were all part of the cast by virtue of being in the shop. It was a new theatrical experience for me. I am not used to this intermingling of artifice and reality. At one point a drunken lady was almost sitting in my lap. Such integration into the spectacle, though very interesting, was not without its alarms, especially with actors addicted to realism.

No one in history was quite as addicted to realism as Peter the Great, a man typical of his people and yet quite exceptional. He was exceptional because he was not only Tsar, but also only a fraction

Caked with snow, this wooden house looks like something from a fairy tale. It is built of slatted wood with richly carved and painted window surrounds. As more and more churches and palaces were built in stone, woodworking craftsmen produced ornate decorations for the windows, balconies and gables of their houses.

under seven foot tall. He was typical because his changes of mood were abrupt and his eccentricity frightening. Nobody grappled with the lethargic immensity of Russia more energetically than he, and no one failed in his battle more gloriously. I accompanied him on a short constitutional walk of a mile, on the deck of his frigate, he striding, I running.

'Hey there, Your Majesty, keep still for a moment. I have to run to keep up with you.'

'Well, you can see I'm in a hurry. So much to do, so little time.'

'But I couldn't catch half of what you were telling me about.'

'You must learn to listen as you run. In any case, it's what people do that's important, not what they say. That's the trouble with Russia, people talk and do nothing. Worse, they talk *in order* to do nothing. Before I took action, the boyars, the so-called great men, thought that it was enough to have a beard to exercise authority. People were conditioned to take beards as a sign of wisdom. Well, I used a couple of strokes of the scissors, and off came the beards. Where was your wisdom then? A little pile of hair on the floor doesn't look much like wisdom does it? Suddenly all the weak chins of the empire were exposed!'

'And you pulled teeth too, didn't you?'

'Yes, I've pulled teeth. And I'll tell you this about dentistry: if the patient screams you're doing it right. On occasion, I've had to do practically everything.'

'Your days must be very full.'

'Life is short. But I don't complain. I studied shipping, learned shipbuilding, became a seaman. Everyone has it in him to be greater than he is. I'd make an excellent churchman, for instance, if I had the time. When I come across a problem, I must know the answer. Facts are essential. That is why I hate beards so. They conceal facts, and merely grow like cabbages, like weeds. Many of the boyars have beards of the mind, which are worse than beards of the chin. Cut 'em off. Get things done. That's how the Tsar should act. But I'm dealing with Russia. God help me.'

CHAPTER FOUR

ADRIFT IN A GIANT LANDSCAPE

The room was dimly lit. Grime streaked the panes of the tall, elegant windows. Light, the off-white daylight of a northern winter, was an intrusion to be kept at bay by long heavy red curtains, sagging in folds on the floor. The furniture was of that intricate, heavy, bulbous kind, with gilded wood and hard, padded upholstery; a table that two men alone could not move and a mirror to reflect oneself in difficulties. The ormolu clock on the mantel was more than an hour slow, battling against the advance of time with a weary tick. On the handsome desk stood an inkwell in the form of a bear. The bear sat on a log with its paw outstretched, which was pushed aside to reveal the ink in the log. The pen was a quill but as a concession to modernity a nib had been fitted. On the walls were landscapes signed by long forgotten artists. Landscapes with cows coming home and stags reflected in the dank forest pools. These were paintings that you accept out of the corner of your eye but never, never look at. A grand piano with yellowed teeth, half of which produced echoes of distant mazurkas, evocations of other times, desperately out of tune.

I was in a Russian hotel room. I was adrift in the giant landscape.

Planes, trains, boats. In a land as large as Russia, all means of transport are pressed into service and extensively used. But the chief means of communication, as in any modern state, is the road – a bewildering variety, from the inter-city race-track of the super highway to the grassy lane of some distant collective.

The roads, in the main, were good, especially the main arteries between big cities. This was surprising, given the size of the countryside and the consequent isolation, and the great extremes of the climate. The journey from Moscow to Tolstoy's home at Yasnaya Polyana takes about five hours in good weather; rather less on the black ice with a Russian driver who talks volubly to his co-pilot all the way. This is one of the most alarming aspects of Soviet transport.

The car for this jaunt was a Chaïka, or Seagull, a massive retro machine which is partly constructed from moulds brought from the now defunct Packard Company in the United States. The doors shut like safes in Fort Knox, with a decisive, irrefutable clunk, and the seats are wide and contourless, sometimes decorated with lace doylys, or antimacassars. The dashboard is rich with the kinds of motif found near the summit of the Empire State Building, traces of scudding cloud and sun ray themes, large red light bulbs glowing fitfully beneath bakelite shades, instruments set in little outbursts of chrome. Small blue cut-glass vases hold bunches of dead flowers, while muddy feet are placed to dry on worn pieces of Turkish or Caucasian carpet.

The drivers of these mobile monuments are so expert at manipulating them, that I swear they could do well in any modern rally. Their continued existence, and effective daily use raises questions about the state of Soviet engineering, but also provides answers. Western motoring journalists are usually rather dismissive of new designs emanating from the Socialist Bloc, conceding points only in the matter of undoubted value. But, of course, these vehicles have those virtues about which journalists are least able to judge. I refer to longevity.

My own cousin, a resident of Leningrad, now in his early eighties, has a Pobieda car from the late forties, a dun-coloured vehicle typical of the period. If you lean on it you have to dust your jacket. He told me that he likes to travel with a passenger who can help him change gear. He has enough strength in his foot to depress the clutch but needs help moving the lever on the steering column. This often gives the impression of a struggle for possession of the wheel. He prefers to do this, not so much because he is feeble but because he has neglected to have the car serviced for the last 400,000 kilometres! No wonder that during the war the Russians preferred to rely on their own crude, tough tanks than on all the subtle, complicated gifts from the West, with so much more in them to go wrong, and, therefore, so much harder to mend.

Russian roads have had to cope with less traffic than Western systems until fairly recently, yet, ironically, the streets are much wider. The main arteries have as many as ten traffic lanes, separated by a continuous grass strip. The inner lanes are reserved for high officials but wherever I travelled, it seemed to me that everyone can become a high official momentarily, if you drive with sufficient bluster and conviction.

The rules for U-Turns and other arabesques are both strict and complex. The signs are painted on the road surface, which means that they are invisible in winter. When it's snowing the driver has the impression of being lost in an ocean of space, his mirror filled with other impatient drivers who know the rules.

Agrophobia is the malady of the day. The atmosphere is claustrophobic in a European city, such as Rome, where you sprint from space to space through an endless river of vehicles. In contrast, in Moscow you may be crossing an enormous highway, with a terrible feeling that the single car still a few hundred yards away is attracted to you as if by a magnet. You are tempted to wave, or leap about, like a shipwrecked sailor, for fear that you are too small for the luxury liner to spot unassisted.

In Georgia, a ferociously independent, hot-headed republic, traffic rules are even more difficult to understand. There's a story about the Russian motorist in Georgia who obediently stops at a red light, only to be hooted at abusively by other drivers, who regale him with raucous shouts, derisive laughter, and gestures indicating his congenital idiocy. All of them go through the red light without looking to the left or right. At the next red light, the same thing happens. The third time, the Russian hesitates, then, believing that this must be some local rule, drives cautiously across the intersection against the red light.

At once there is an ear-piercing whistle, and the Georgian policeman, with a patent leather moustache, imperiously beckons him to the curb.

'You went through a red light,' he snaps, as he produces his book of tickets, and begins writing.

'Yes,' shouts the indignant Russian.

'Why?' asks the policeman, still writing.

'Everybody else does it.'

The policeman takes a moment to inscribe the car's number on his document.

'You've read your Highway Code?' he inquires, softly.

'Of course.'

The policeman indicates the chaotic traffic with his pencil.

'They haven't,' he explains.

Space there may be in the streets, but the appartments are cramped and overcrowded. There has been a housing crisis ever since the war

The wide, wide streets of Gori (top left) and Volgograd (top right). Volgograd, then called Stalingrad, was almost completely destroyed in 1943 and has since been rebuilt on the hillside overlooking the River Volga. It stretches for about 80 kilometres along the river. Massive flights of granite steps descend from the town centre to the edge of the river (above left). On the bank there is a river station (above right) where ferries leave for Moscow, Astrakhan and Rostov-on-Don.

This huge statue, representing the Motherland (top left) stands at the top of Mamaiev Hill in Volgograd, and is part of a giant war memorial. The mill (top right) shattered by gun fire has been preserved as a relic of the battle. It was used as the headquarters for a military unit. Soldiers (above) change the guard at the war memorial, Volgograd.

and the pressure on family life is acute. Newly weds often live with parents and surviving grandparents, and so all phases of life are squeezed together in an uncomfortable proximity. Babies are yelling, while young parents yearn for some privacy, older parents try to work and grandparents hope for silence and rest.

The apartment buildings, which were almost invariably thrown up in haste, are not the best advertisements for Soviet workmanship. Whereas tractors, cars, rolling stock seem to last for ever, the buildings show their age. Surfaces are poorly finished, joints don't always meet where they are supposed to. Elevators shudder, and often stop with an ominous drumbeat. The plywood interiors are rich in graffiti, not so much an expression of artistic inclination as of the impatience of the occupants while waiting to be rescued.

Even if home life is not ideal, there are saving graces. Even families of extremely modest means have cottages, or at least shacks in the countryside, where they can enjoy nature, and all the pleasures of solitude which it offers. Here they can cultivate their own fruit, vegetables, and flowers, and contribute to the contemporary proverb, 'Nothing in the shops, everything on the table.'

Western influence of various sorts is widespread. It even extends to drum majorettes. I saw with amazement that the young Lithuanian girls mirrored their high-stepping American models, with that cock-eyed parody of military uniform. It was just as if these Baltic maidens had come straight from the football field at Texas High, or from the boards of Radio City Music Hall some 40 years ago. They had the glossy long boots, very short skirts, showing a great deal of leg, and cowboy hats perched on bouffant coiffures. No doubt their jaws were masticating gum strictly in tempo. They strutted with the same toothpaste grin and the same shake of the buttocks, and they waved in the air the same sticks with the candy floss tops. Only the spectators were a little less infected with enthusiasm. They merely clapped.

The other influence are the pop combos which make most restaurants places of torture to those who merely wish to eat. Conversation is out of the question as the decibels mount far beyond

Looking very like their counterparts in London or New York, these Russian teenagers posed for me on a bridge over one of Leningrad's many canals.

the level of hysteria, and the strobe-lights stammer out their invitation to nervous disease. It is difficult to know why this, the most nonsensical expression of Western high spirits, should be the one widespread export of our way of life. While our politicians utter pious platitudes about freedom, one aspect of it, the freedom to break the sound barrier while jumping about, has really taken root among the young in the Eastern Bloc.

A pretty little girl in Leningrad followed me in the street, muttering something about Wrangel. I could not understand why a 15-year-old student should wish to know something about Wrangel, who was a White Russian general engaged in struggles with the Bolsheviks in the early days of the Revolution, some 70 years ago.

It turned out, on closer investigation, that she was eager to enlist my help, as a foreigner with hard currency, to buy her a pair of Wranglers. These, far from being followers of a half-forgotten Tsarist general, are merely blue jeans.

Most tourists see Moscow and Leningrad, but have neither the time nor, perhaps, the inclination to go much further afield. Curiously enough, the further you go from the centres of power, the more normal and relaxed the life of ordinary people tends to become. Although air travel has revolutionised communications, the train is still a stately and restful method of getting around, especially at night, because the wider gauge makes a more comfortable journey. Sometimes, in winter, the trains are overheated, but you are quickly grateful for this.

When you get off the train, you notice that not only is the distance between the train and the platform considerable, but there is the added hazard that the edge of the platform slopes down towards the rails. With ice and snow around, it makes the negotiating of this hazard practically impossible without help, even from little old ladies who are used to these conditions.

Once, on the night train to Novgorod, a square woman in a dark blue uniform came plodding down the train holding aloft what was unmistakably a dripping enema-bag. Later on, I saw the bag hanging

The Cathedral of St. Sophia (1045–52), Novgorod, was built by Grand Prince Vladimir, son of Yaroslav the Wise, as the principal church of the town and coronation church of its princes. The huge monument outside the cathedral was erected in 1862 during Alexander II's reign, to celebrate the millenary of Russia. The 129 sculptures on it represent all the great heroes of Russia.

in the toilet, and suspect it was used to draw hot water out of the central heating system, for the manufacture of instant tea. Perhaps I am wrong, but curiously enough it left me with no thirst for tea for the rest of the journey.

Novgorod, even under snow, is a most impressive city. Had she not traded with the West at a time when such activities without permission from the Tsar led to an automatic death sentence? Novgorod was, in fact, a Hansa city, linked with cities such as Hamburg and Lübeck in the great trading chain, and as such was Russia's door to the West long before Peter the Great built St. Petersburg as the window.

The icons and artefacts in Novgorod are of surprising beauty, as is the Cathedral of St. Sophia, dating from a few years before the Norman Conquest of England. The walls of the Kremlin are built of the traditional red brick of the region, a warm, glowing colour quite different to that of other Russian churches. Inside of one of the most beautiful turrets, there is perhaps the most deafening of all Soviet restaurants. The ancient walls shook to the stamp of the feet of Finnish octogenarian tourists in their search for the dizzy irresponsibility of youth.

Kiev, that other even more ancient city, is at its best with the rustle of spring. Nature seems to sprout amongst the streets and boulevards, trembling leaves cast shadows on the sidewalks, petals blown hither and thither by the breeze. There is a feeling of exultation, faces creased in the glare of the sunlight, steps lightened by the excitement of fair weather after foul.

The landscape is both majestic and initimate; hedgerows, shady lanes, puddles, fat geese wheezing around them like toy steam-engines, the endless prattle of pigs and their young, clean linen and freckled faces and stray golden hairs catching the rays of the sun.

It is this understated opulence of nature which makes the tragedy of Chernobyl so very bitter. Contaminated crops, mile upon mile of inedible fruit rotting in the orchards. Empty houses with doors creaking on their hinges. Uneaten meals on the tables. The poisoned earth. The serenity of the skies and the green of the grass deriding the sinister foolishness of man. Spring kept the appointment, as usual. It was man who did not.

On Palm Sunday (or Reed Sunday as the Russians call it), we were waiting in the grounds of Kiev Cathedral for the Archbishop to arrive. It was a beautiful day and suddenly my wife and I smiled at each other with the purest affection. It was just one of those special moments. An old lady stepped out of the crowd and said to my wife, 'Here one does not smile.' When she visited a church in Moscow, and crossed herself in the Catholic manner, she was reprimanded once again, this time by an old man: 'Not that way. Don't you know any better? Here we cross ourselves from right to left.'

The survival of religion in a Marxist land is not really an anomaly, since Russia is devoted to her past. When I was looking down on the Georgian city of Tbilisi from the hills above, I noticed mosques and churches of all denominations cheek by jowl, all open and all in operation. The official with me was a Communist and an unbeliever. 'Don't bother me with that old stuff,' he said. 'It's all nonsense. I know nothing about it, nor do I want to.' But I went on speculating idly. A Georgian and an Armenian church stood almost side by side. What was the difference between them? The languages and alphabets were different, but how did their belief differ? Suddenly my atheist companion turned to me. 'I'll tell you the difference. One believes in the Immaculate Conception of the Virgin and the other doesn't. One lot cross themselves with three fingers going from left to right and the other lot with two fingers from right to left. Now, is there anything else you'd like to know?'

Whatever the attitude of Soviet authority, religion, memory, even superstition are inextricably intertwined in the Russian imagination. That same good unbelieving Georgian official was with me when the poet Yevtushenko and I visited the tomb of Boris Pasternak. Solemnly, the Georgian took a little wine and sprinkled

With my wife Hélène on the steps of Kiev Cathedral on 'Reed' Sunday which is celebrated as Palm Sunday in the West.

With the poet Yevtushenko I visited the home and grave of Boris Pasternak, author of Doctor Zhivago, *in the small village of Peredelkino, a traditional home for writers and poets. Pasternak died here in May 1960 and was buried in the local cemetery.*

it reverentially on the tomb, for this was an old burial custom, a mark of respect to the departed shade of a noble writer. Yevtushenko himself, quite apart from being a thoroughly contemporary fellow, is also a repository of old ceremonies, lore, custom and superstition. He lives in the village of Peredelkino, where Pasternak made his home, a place devoted to writers and artists. Yevtushenko took me to the village church where a service was taking place. The congregation in an Orthodox Church is always rather more mobile than a Catholic or Protestant one since there are no pews. We watched old people kissing the fabric of the church itself in sheer religious fervour. Yevtushenko was excited, too. He rushed over to me, wanting to know the Christian names and patronymics of my dead parents. I had to think for a minute, for this mysterious request had taken me by surprise. Then he wrote the names on a piece of paper, disappeared into the back regions of the church and came back with two hard little cakes. These had been blessed by the local priest and had thereby acquired some significant association with the memory of my parents, and if I ate them the next morning on an empty stomach certain intercessions, about which I was none too clear, would take place in the next world.

In deference to the wishes of the great poet, I woke early in my hotel the next morning and looked at those cakes which were now as hard as stone. No doubt the loss of a few teeth was regarded as an essential part of the sacrifice. But suddenly I thought that my parents, wherever they were, would forgive me if I decided that the loss of valuable teeth could not be a prerequisite for thinking of them. So I contented myself with a moment of meditation, during which I imagined my parents laughing at all this, and I smiled as I dropped the rock-like cakes into the wastepaper basket.

I have already touched briefly on the character of Soviet hotels, which range from the time-honoured to the ultra-modern, passing through the fidgety gothic style of the Stalin period. Tradition is well represented by hotels such as the National and Metropole in Moscow, and the Astoria and Europeïskaya Gostinnitsa in Lenin-

Tbilisi (top left), the capital of Georgia, is one of the oldest cities in the world. Nowadays, it is a thriving industrial city. The Archbishop's residence (top right) is in the old town. The fruit and vegetable market (above) is one of five large markets in Tbilisi.

grad. Some years ago they still gave you keys with metal discs the size of plates attached, not only impossible to take away in error, but also impossible to force into your pocket. The number of the room was engraved on the disc, and also, very faintly around the rim, the name of the hotel – Grand Hotel de L'Europe, St. Petersbourg. Those were the days, or rather 'Ah, c'était la Belle Epoque!'

Habitable Stalin Mausoleums are usually met in the provinces, apart from stray examples such as the gargantuan Moskva and Rossiya. The many entrances are distinguished by points of the compass, each a short taxi ride from the other, and a search for the swimming pool is liable to leave you in acres of kitchen among cooks eager for company from the outside world.

The more modern style of hotel is scarcely more successful, especially in the bathrooms. A rapid movement in the bathtub, which is part of a pre-cast element, creates an effect throughout the room resembling an earth tremor quite high on the Richter scale.

There is also a general mistrust of electricity, since everything is unplugged when not in use. In one hotel I stayed in, it was impossible to use the refrigerator and the television at the same time, so there were often awkward choices to make. Do you drink tepid lager while watching the European Cup final or do you drink iced lager, and stare at the dead tube, imagining what is going on.

But on the whole, you learn to live with these peculiarities, which become almost endearing in the end. The female concierges who sit, barricaded behind their desks on every floor, observing the comings and goings to and from the elevators like spy-satellites, are at first rather forbidding, with prejudice dictating the nature of their functions. After a few days, however, they become warm-hearted mother figures, sharing your outrage every time an electrical fixture blows a fuse, and procuring you mineral water or pamphlets about hydro-electric plants in Azerbaijan in the middle of the night.

The human element, once again, always transcends the material, given time. We arrived in Volgograd, the Stalingrad that was, at two in the morning, after our plane had been delayed in taking off from Simferopol in the Crimea. Our limousine only reached the hotel minutes before three. The restaurant had waited until one, but then had been unable to continue its service. Nevertheless, in conjunction with the lady concierges, they had prepared tea, soup, a mountain of hors d'oeuvres, assuming that we had not dined. Such kindness dispensed to total strangers is typical of the inherent fellow feeling which makes them formidable in times of war, and fulfils some of the more spiritual precepts of Communist theory, which could be called Christian, or many other things in similar circumstances elsewhere.

The general level of honesty has always seemed to me extremely high, as is the degree of altruism. In Leningrad I was desperate for some Western shaving soap, of which there was none in the hotel store, nor in the perfumery in the Nevsky Prospekt. I asked the doorman to find a taxi. He assumed a mysterious look, and talked to a friend. The friend beckoned us to follow him. He led us not to a taxi but to a coach, with about 50 seats. 'Get in,' he commanded.

My wife and I asked, 'In here?'

'I've got Hungarians. They've had a late night.'

We drove to a huge hotel in the outskirts of the city, on the Baltic. There was no shaving cream. It was amusing to look through the first floor window of the supermarket, and to see a huge red coach waiting for just the two of us.

'Well?' asked the driver.

'No luck.'

'I have an idea.'

He drove us over to the Leningrad Hotel, another twenty minutes away.

'What about your Hungarians?' I asked en route.

He made a gesture of a throat being slit.

I said, 'Forget about the shaving soap. I can always borrow some.'

No answer. He just went on driving.

At the Leningrad, I found what I had been looking for.

He smiled with satisfaction, and drove back to our point of departure as though the coach had been transformed into a Ferrari.

The great cathedral at Yevpatoriya (top) was built in 1892 to commemorate all those who died in the Crimean War. To the left stands the mosque of the Old City (1552–7). The town is now a centre for convalescing children, and a popular resort where people enjoy strolling along the seafront promenades in the mild climate.

There were no Hungarians waiting when we got back. He heaved a sigh of relief, which turned to annoyance when I offered him what a taxi would have cost as compensation.

'I didn't take you for money,' he said, 'but in order to find you shaving soap.'

A great deal is always made in the Western press about alleged corruption in the Soviet Union. Some official in an Asian republic has been discovered cornering the market in nylons, or occasionally someone is even shot for making huge profits on the side, but we never seem to equate these reports with the far more numerous shenanigans in the open markets of the West.

It stands to reason that any bureaucracy as huge and complicated as that of the Soviet Union is bound to attract those tendencies towards larceny in human nature. But these tendencies do not bear comparison with the exploits of the share-pushers and entrepreneurs – laundering funds, and diverting them into their own labyrinthine pockets – which we read about daily, equating freedom with indiscriminate opportunity.

Certainly on the lowest level, the ordinary citizen of the Soviet Union is strikingly free of criminal initiative. There is very little likelihood of being mugged over there, and even murder is not a frequent solution to aggravation. So it's surprising to find that no windscreen-wipers or bath-plugs are safe from pilferers. Perhaps driving through the snow while clearing the windscreen with a rag, and taking a bath with your heel jammed in the plug hole, are small prices to pay for a society with fewer serious crimes.

Air travel is becoming more and more accessible to all stratas of society. The planes are always full, and while being rather utilitarian, they are certainly as comfortable as local lines elsewhere. The armrests are movable, and the back of the seats collapse forwards if unoccupied, so it is sometimes possible to create a little more room than there really is. My translator in Russia is a delightful fellow, both taller and stouter than I, and with whom I have had to

After a performance of Shakespeare's Richard III *at the Georgian National Theatre in Tbilisi, the cast surprised me with a 64th birthday party. My neighbour is Ramaz Chikvadze one of Georgia's greatest actors. I tried some wines from the Crimea at an official wine-tasting at Massandra (above) – a far cry from the Hospice de Beaune.*

A statue of Stalin at the Stalin museum in Gori (top). This small two-roomed house in the suburbs of Gori (above) is Stalin's birthplace and is now a museum. The house was owned by a poor shopkeeper who rented one of the rooms to a shoemaker, Stalin's father. The family lived here until 1883 in total poverty.

travel far and wide. Aeroflot, with a blend of humour and charity, gave us three complementary seats between us. The gesture was much appreciated.

The new Soviet airbus on international lines is a big step forward, and seems to owe nothing to other designs. You enter the passenger space by a long flight of stairs. It is as if, in the Boeing 747, everyone were seated on the upper level. People often appear, usually searching for elusive toilets, at the top of these palatial stairs, while in flight. The seats are extremely comfortable and the relationship between tables and seats is wonderfully generous for the corpulent. I have not had to indulge in my usual habit of wearing a tie purchased in India while in flight, so that food dropped on it in the course of a most uncomfortable lunch will only add to the complication of the design, and my clumsiness will pass unnoticed. The standard of design and the level of silence on such flights are at least up to the standards set elsewhere. Gone are the days when plastic covers were dispensed before take-off to wrap round your fountain-pen, in case the altitude caused it to leak in your pocket.

Gori, in Georgia, is the last ditch of Stalinism. It was here that the discredited architect of the dark age of Communism was born. His birthplace was a meagre hut, dignified but rendered ludicrous at the same time by a kind of mini-Parthenon built over it, in order to lend the simple structure a degree of solemnity. From a distance it looks as though the neo-Greek shell is suckling the cottage, which huddles like Romulus and Remus beneath the maternal shadow of the wolf.

    The only surviving monument to Stalin is near the railway station, atop a high column. Wherever you stand, the face is always in the shade, which is finally as it should be. You have to refer to the name at the foot of the column to find out who it is.

Georgia is a republic of some 6 million lively people with a culture entirely its own, a national theatre with a style and vigour comparable to no other, and a language which lends itself to explosive passion and to lilting tenderness. It is the country of opulence. In the five large open markets in the capital, Tbilisi, there is everything in abundance, from fruit and flowers, to meat and groceries. I bought seeds there which have flourished in Switzerland. It is not often, in the Soviet Union, that you can witness such an expression of plenty. And yet, return to the hotel, and you once again fall victim to the absurd, wasteful system of centralisation. Some civil servant, who must be off his food, seems to set the menus for the whole country according to what is available in Moscow, and dictates to all the different tentacles of the giant Intourist chain what tourists may or may not eat.

After my visit to the open market, I returned for lunch at the hotel.

'What's on today?' I asked the waiter.

The menu is not to be trusted. A work of the imagination. In Leningrad I even found, under Today's Specials, the word 'Bread.'

'Today,' he answered, 'there is fish and there is meat.'

'Yes, what kind of meat?'

He looked at me with rather hurt surprise. 'Meat,' he said.

So I sent him off to the kitchen to inquire about the meat. He returned beaming.

'There's a nice piss biff, and there is pig.'

That sort of approach was not encouraging. It seemed inexcusable in a town of such superabundance that the cuisine should be so poor and so limited. In private homes, on the other hand, the food was delectable – salads, cold and hot meats, delicious breads, fruits of all kinds – served with style and skill in rooms perfumed with flowers. It made the surly hotel fare very hard to bear.

Distribution and supply of food is obviously a great problem throughout Russian cities. Some markets have now opened where peasant and townsfolk are directly in contact, and this has done something to alleviate the shortages. But the State planners are not defeated yet and continue to tie diabolical knots in the long bureaucratic lines of the centralised distribution process. You inquire about eggs in the appropriate shop.

Novosibirsk is the new town of Siberia (top). During the last war, factories situated near the front were dismantled and moved to Novosibirsk and reassembled. As a result the town's industrial output increased five times, and this expansion has continued since 1945. Visitors to Siberia are surprised to see air-conditioners (above) but the weather is as hot in the summer as it is cold in the winter.

The clowns take the ring at the Moscow Circus.

'Nothing today. Try round the corner, next street but one.'

'No, no, we've been there already. Nothing doing.'

'No eggs there? Well, I don't know what to suggest. Perhaps you could take the train to the country ...'

So you do, and there, a mere two miles from the city gates, right there on the platform of the country station, is an old lady with hundreds of eggs that she can't get rid of.

There is no sense of diffusion, no idea how to make elementary commerce spread evenly through the people at large. I have been to restaurants that run out of beer, or wine, yet there is a stall selling these drinks in the road outside. Sometimes you just summon the waiter and point him to the door, and he goes and buys it for you.

There is a strange inability to match talent to performance in the Soviet Union, and you can understand with compassion the problems which confront Mr Gorbachev and his fellow reformers. One of the human rights near to the Soviet heart is the right to work, in the sense that work is a prerequisite for the maintenance of human dignity. When you consider the prevalence of massive unemployment which surrounds us, with the attendant degradation of the human spirit, you know that, however one may quarrel with certain Soviet concepts of the rights of Man, here they have a point, and a valid one.

And yet even here, one cannot avoid noticing anomalies in the practical application of their theories.

I remember seeing an athletic young man engaged in impaling autumn leaves on a pointed stick in a park, and through the railings you could also see three stocky grandmothers having trouble in starting a steam-roller.

Theories should arise from practicality, because practicality simply cannot rise from theory. You want proof?

My three outstanding restaurants in Russia, worthy of crossed forks or stars in any guide, have one thing in common, independence from Intourist, and the dictatorship of some faraway gastronomic puritan. The first is the Old Fortress, Staraya Krepust, in Taganrog, on the

Sea of Azov, Chekhov's birthplace. The fish has avoided the fate of others. It is uncentralised, fresh, and filled with cabbage by a brilliant cook, who gave us one of the great culinary experiences of a lifetime.

The second is the Ukraine, in Yevpatoriya, in the Crimea. It is a pleasant town with endless sand beaches, now a centre for the convalescence of ailing children. The trams are all painted with the Soviet equivalent of Disney characters, and there is an atmosphere of pleasant fairy-tale improbability about the whole place, down to the strange salt-water swans. These birds float around near the harbours, catching fish, with completely different tactics from the dignified lacustrine birds which have inspired ballet dancers to tasteful evocations in the past. It is only right that in a fairy-tale world, the Ukraine should not only have excellent food, but the greatest caramel ice-cream ever invented.

The third is in the martyr city of Volgograd. It has two great advantages, fresh fish from the Volga, well cooked, and an unamplified piano, discreetly played instead of the howling static and masticating crackle of a combo. It is called 'Neptun', as strange a name for a river as the swans were oddities at sea.

It is evident that small countries are easier to run than larger ones. Before World War I, Finland was part of Russia since she was seized from Sweden. Finland today is like a well-ordered room, compared with the straggling warehouse of the Soviet Union. This is true even of the small republics, Latvia, Lithuania and Estonia, as well as the cluster in the south, Armenia, Georgia and Azerbaijan, and further to the east, Kazakhstan, Uzbekistan, Kirghizia and the others, as well as the various autonomous territories. First of all, they speak their own languages, and the Russians usually don't. Their habits, problems, and religions are different.

In Lithuania, for instance, there may be the odd statue of Lenin, but the Catholic churches are full on Sunday, as they are in Poland. Georgia we have already discussed, but it is true even in the Crimea, now an integral part of the Ukraine and a Russian-speaking area, that there is a feeling of cohesion and identity by virtue of the fact

One of the stranger sights at Yevpatoriya was a group of sea-faring swans. All the brightly coloured trams in Yevpatoriya are painted with cartoon characters.

The Palace of the Khans (top), now the Historical and Archaeological Museum – at Bakshisaray, north-west of Yalta. This was the old capital of the Tartar Khans. The 15th century palace was destroyed and then rebuilt by Catherine the Great in 1787. (Above) The mosque in Tbilisi.

that it is to all intents and purposes an island. It is in the vastness of Russia itself, and the even more unimaginable size of Siberia that the colours of existence tend to run, overlap, and lose their definition as in a water-colour sketch.

Siberia has a bad reputation, thanks to the media. Dostoyevsky, Solzhenitsyn, and the tragic multitude have disappeared into its mists. In our imagination it resembles a series of gulags set in the most atrocious climate, miles from anywhere and miles from each other. Its music is the moaning of winds and the choral howling of wolves. Yet, Britain had its Siberia too, not 150 years ago. Look at it today. It is called Australia.

If it is true that the centre of gravity in the matter of human ingenuity and its industrial application is gradually shifting from the Atlantic to the Pacific, and that weary old Europe and the eastern seaboard of the United States are loosening their grip on vital technologies – surrendering their ancient privileges to the American western seaboard, to Japan, China, South Korea, Taiwan, Hong Kong, Singapore and other industrialised zones with exceptional talent and/or cheaper labour – then it is also true that an undertow can be felt pulling the Russian fulcrum east towards the Pacific.

Siberia is both a continual temptation and a permanent challenge. It is immensely wealthy, but its wealth is tantalising, since well over half of the land mass is subject to permafrost. This means that only the very surface of the soil thaws out. Under the surface, it remains frozen. And yet, in the short summer, it can be very hot indeed, gnats and mosquitos from the coniferous forests making life a misery. The beaches on proud rivers are covered in bikini-clad figures and young people playing strenuous games with balls and bats.

The people tend to smile. Musicians say they are the greatest audience there is, actors say they are the greatest public. It stands to reason. Like the inhabitants of Iceland, they are completely unspoiled, and keen to witness any artistic manifestation, and be ebulliently grateful for it, too. It is a land of wild surprises.

Near the largest city, Novosibirsk, there is an artificial town, built entirely for men and women of science. It is called Akademgorodok, meaning academic hamlet. It looks like any contemporary garden city, half lost in trees. We hoped to shoot a few feet of film there, but conscious of the well-fuelled Soviet reputation for secrecy, we hadn't much hope.

'Being foreigners, I presume the nuclear centre is what interests you most,' the professor in charge of public relations said. 'Come on. We'll stroll over there and see what is possible. It's a pity we didn't know you were coming.'

The building is large and modern without being revolutionary. We found the senior members of the staff in the conference room, sitting casually round a huge table in their shirt-sleeves, sipping coffee. The head of the centre, an extremely shy young man, Academician Srinsky, did not say much. His brilliance was evident, but so was his reticence in communicating it. His deputy, rather older and garrulous, did all the communicating which was necessary.

'I don't know why, but whenever architects build for scientists, they always believe we need conference rooms, with marble walls and huge tables. In fact, when we are in the grip of a technical discussion, we forget where we are, on a walk in the woods, using adjacent basins in the men's room, lining up in the canteen. If the discussion is sufficiently compelling or divisive, in all three places. So this, despite the wood sculpture of our founding father on the wall, and the huge stucco profile of Lenin, has become simply the coffee room.'

They were a cheerful lot, these men of science, explaining, with the help of beautifully produced pamphlets, the commercial uses of nuclear power, including remote and exportable techniques of killing off dangerous impurities in wheat. Nuclear power is such a paradoxical subject that I have no clear picture in my untechnical mind of what is and what is not possible without danger, other than to be struck by the fact that so many people outraged by the drama of Chernobyl are those who also believe that the same risks, served up differently, are vital for our security.

All I can report constitutes neither a defence nor a condemnation of nuclear power, but merely a description of what I saw. We were

The space-rocket must wait until after the game has finished.

The crêche at Novosibirsk where tiny gardeners tackle the irrigation problem.

allowed to watch a laser beam at work, in a sophisticated experiment in an atomic particle accelerator. On film it looked like a huge blue cornea. In contrast to the Western habit of farming out the manufacture of articles to large commercial interests, the boys at Akademgorodok have built their own factory on the nuclear site, capable of building what is necessary as a one-off, artisanal piece of sophisticated equipment.

I had a feeling that the relation between pure science and industry is neither a clear, nor a mutually dependent one in the Soviet mind. It is as though there exist temples of pure science, which are of a very high level, but that the practical application of the knowledge leaves a lot to be desired.

Be that as it may, I was moved to tell them that if Hollywood were ever tempted to put them on film in some extravaganza in which a Superyank single-handedly sets back Soviet science a decade, they would have to be subject to recasting. They were not nearly grim enough, nor were they in uniform. 'Why!' I declared, 'You people aren't even what we're used to in Moscow.'

'Why do you think we are here?' asked one professor, grinning from ear to ear. 'The weather is sometimes terrible, but it's worth it. *Anything* to be away from Moscow – if you want to get anything done, that is.'

'Do you ever go to America?' asked another professor as we were taking our leave.

I said I did.

'I have a friend there,' he said, 'a professor at Stanford. We are linked in friendship not only by our abiding interest in the same branch of science, but even more by our passion for breeding cocker spaniels. Would it be too much to ask you to phone whenever you are next over there to tell him that Barbara has had seven.' And he gave me the number on a card.

Whatever the final judgment on matters nuclear, the men engaged in this industry are like men anywhere else, with the anchor of a discipline, interested in everything developing around them, of open mind.

Not far away is one of many crêches for the children of scientific parents, both of whom work. These are not at all what hostile propagandists affirm to be efforts of the powers that be to control children, and destroy the family in favour of that mysterious miscreant, the State. Children are fetched by their parents on Friday nights, and stay with them throughout the weekend, returning to the company of other children for the rest of the week. Since children need both their parents and the company of other children, the sense of pervasive equilibrium is both pleasant and reassuring, as is the relaxed attitude of the ladies who run the place.

Irkutsk is a large town, dating from the early 17th century, very near the border with Outer Mongolia. It is memorable historically as the place to which some of the plotters of the Decembrist movement against Tsar Nicholas I in 1825, were sent, notably Prince Trubetskoy, whose young wife won the admiration of society by accompanying her husband to his distant place of exile. Today it is an industrial city, an important stopping place on the Trans-Siberian railway.

Just as Novosibirsk, sometimes nicknamed the Chicago of Siberia, has Akademgorodok in its immediate vicinity, so Irkutsk has another extraordinay feature a short boat ride away from it.

Lake Baykal is certainly one of the most surprising places one could hope to visit on the face of the earth. It is the deepest lake in the world, so clear, so unpolluted that it is possible to scoop water from its surface with a glass, and to drink it without fear. It is freezing and utterly delicious. The banks of the lake are reminiscent of many places, Switzerland, Scotland, Canada, and even the French riviera. Café-au-lait cows wander in fields full of daisies and buttercups, wooden chalets abound, and, at times, mists hang in the air like smears on the crystalline clarity of the water.

In the Crimea we saw salt-water swans; here, there are fresh-water seals. How they came here, and adapted themselves to local conditions is a mystery, but they sit on stones, cheerful, whiskered, glossy creatures, clapping their flappers in approval of nature around them. There are over 100 species of fish, animal, bird and insect

All ribbons, bows and games at play-school in Siberia.

Lake Baykal (top) is a two-hour boat trip from Irkutsk. It is the ancient, sacred sea of the Tunguz tribes and is the oldest and deepest lake in the world. The countryside surrounding the lake is like France, Switzerland or even the heart of Quebec.

which are exclusive to this immediate area, including such extraordinary creatures as the so-called oil fish. It's the size of a red mullet, and conceives its young in a womb, and gives birth to fish instead of roe! The lake seems to hold the secrets of our prehistoric links to life in primeval bogs, and probably has much more to reveal beneath its pristine surface.

The impressions of the Soviet Union are infinite in number, and we only scratched the surface during our brief four months in search of the tormented past and the present fraught with contention and tremendous interest.

There are reconstructions of strange courtship habits in Turkic Kirghizia, where men pursue girls, all of them on wild part-Arab horses, with small heads and mad eyes, like those in the paintings by Delacroix and Géricault. The girls have a head start, and it is the men's aim to kiss them at the gallop. If they succeed, the courtship is abruptly over. If they fail, they have to gallop back to base, with a head start, pursued by the girls armed with long cruel whips to lash their slothful suitors. Obviously, the process is not as arbitrary as it seems. Marriage-minded girls allow themselves to be caught, while masochistic men are not worth having anyway.

The great table delicacy in these parts is a paté resembling a Japanese transistor crushed under the weight of a passing truck, with all the little circuits baked into a flat brown mould. It was, I was told, made of the entrails of new-born horses. This hardly surprised me since I had recently been on the other side of the great Tien Shan

mountains, in China, where the local gourmet dish is a wobbling aspic containing oblong black objects of no particular taste, but with a consistency of phlegm. This addictive delight turned out to be the pads from the bottom of camels' feet. When I asked the governor of Gansu, the poorest of China's provinces, what happened to the rest of the camel, he made a dismissive gesture, 'O, that no goo' to eat,' he said.

The red brick of Novgorod, the white or grey patina of the oldest Russian churches, the blackened wood of ancient buildings, the Victorian and Edwardian gothic of the melancholy Italianate villas in Yalta, displaying the pallor of ill-health and fin-de-siècle decadence, the soulless administrative cathedrals of Stalinism, the mint-green, ochre, mustard, cerulean, tints of Russian houses in Leningrad and Moscow, the Palladian style of civic palaces in the provinces, the plump little places of worship, with golden onion domes, or dark blue ones, peppered with stars, the grander churches, of unsparing wealth, peasant cottages with elaborately carved window-sills and shutters; they are all distinctively national in style, and cannot be mistaken for buildings anywhere else.

They find an abstract echo in the romantic sweep of Tchaikovsky and the fractured musical prose of Mussorgsky, the shafts of refracted Chékhovian light and the ferocious beam of Dostoyevsky, the intensity of prayer and the depths of debasements. It is a land where the soul is spoken of unashamedly, as there is no other word for that battleground where gluttony and abstinence, good and evil, right and wrong clash so consistently.

A final Russian proverb: Praise God, but do not neglect the Devil.

It is perhaps just a quarrel between old friends, the fallen angel was an angel once. Before his fall, when all was dazzling white, God could not recognize himself. It needed black for distinctions to be made, for lines to be drawn. And for the creation of grey, the only area in which human beings can breathe, tempted permanently by light, like moths, or the darkness, like snakes, but unable to live elsewhere but the battleground, the home of personality, of soul.

A group of children mount guard outside the tomb of the unknown soldier at Irkutsk (top). In 1825, the Decembrists – a group of noble revolutionaries, mostly still serving officers – failed in their attempt at a palace coup and the ringleaders were executed. Others were exiled to Siberia. Prince Sergei Trubetskoy was exiled to this house in Irkutsk (above).

This huge statue of Chekhov (top) stands in Gagarin Park, Yalta. Yalta (above) lies on the southernmost tip of the Crimean peninsular and is a popular health resort because of its mild climate and sheltered coastline. The dramatic cliffs of the Crimean coastline (right). Swallow's Nest (top right) sits perched on the cliffs, near Yalta. The castle was built in 1912 by a German oil magnate, and is now a restaurant.

View from the operations room of the Yalta conference. The abacus, as seen on the desk, is still widely used in Russia today.

In the courtyard of the Livadia Palace, the summer residence of the Tsars, near Yalta. Stalin, Roosevelt and Churchill met here in February 1945 for the Yalta conference. The map shows the European situation in 1945 (above left). A view of the conference room (above right) from Roosevelt's viewpoint.

CHAPTER FIVE

A SENSE OF WHAT SHOULD BE

You learn from your mistakes, Lenin used to insist. The image of Lenin is stamped on Soviet society. It is a face you never forget: the domed intellectual forehead, the shrewd penetrating glance with something eastern in it, a half-smile not really confirmed by the eyes, the thin face jutting aggressively forward to the little pointed beard. Finding him everywhere I travelled in Russia, I was determined to include him in my interviews.

The suggestion made the high Soviet official in Gosteleradio, the State Television Organization, turn pale. After a moment he said, 'Mr Ustinov, it is as though you were asking the Vatican for their technical assistance, to put *your* version of Jesus on the screen.'

I saw his point, understanding all too clearly the place Lenin occupies on the altarpiece of the hierarchy. I suggested Lenin aged 23, before he had achieved anything palpable. This I was allowed to do, helped by the admirable young actor Orlov.

I came upon him on a flight of rickety stairs.

'Ulyanov?' I asked softly. He had not assumed the name of Lenin yet. He was writing, using his kneecaps as a desk.

On hearing his name, he handed me the document, and asked briskly, 'Will I be allowed to go to my room before we leave?'

'Leave? Where to?'

'You are arresting me, aren't you?'

'No.'

He seemed relieved, but then grew wary.

'Then, how did you know my name?' he inquired.

Once he was sure that I was a bona fide foreigner, I asked him what his aims in life were. He replied that in the immediate future his ambitions were to go abroad for a while, to widen his experience. He held out high hopes of this, since he had only been turned down once so far. And, he added, 'It is my hope not to spend too much time in prison, despite the excellent quality of the people one finds there.'

The statue of Lenin outside the Finland Station, Leningrad. It was here that Lenin and other exiles arrived in 1917.

*Lenin's study in the Smolny Institute. The building was originally a boarding school for
daughters from noble families, founded by Catherine II. During the October revolution, the
Revolutionary War Committee worked from there. Lenin and Trotsky lived there until
the Soviet Government was moved to Moscow in 1918. The name comes from
smola (tar) because this was once the site of the tar and pitch stores of Peter I's
shipbuilding industry.*

Of his eventual ambitions, he spoke quite unexcitedly about world revolution. When I expressed surprise at such a casual way of addressing vast problems, he fixed me suddenly with an intense stare and addressed me in clipped and irrefutable accents as though I were not so much a man as a moderate sized rally.

'You look at me as if I were merely an idealist, with my head in the clouds. But I travel the hard road of experience. We will all make mistakes. But even if we make 10,000 mistakes for every 100 correct solutions, our revolution will be great and invincible. For the first time, the vast majority of working people will build a new life themselves. *You* do not understand how we can succeed, but I do not understand how we can fail.'

The mistakes have been made and I see now the ghost of Lenin beginning to count reasons to justify them. After the terrible years of Stalin and the epoch of doctrinaire Marxism, Lenin's hands, perhaps, begin a tentative clap for Mikhail Gorbachev.

Learning is a hard process, hard to institute, hard to grapple with, but also hard to reverse. The names change and are erased from the memory. The old city of Tsaritsyn became Stalingrad but now it is Volgograd. The Tsars and Stalin did their damage, and then they were no more. The Volga is more constant. When we went to film in the Stalin Museum in his home town of Gori, I worried about what the locals might say about the sharp and bitter things I had written in my commentary. Stalin was, after all, one of the most powerful men in the world and was, moreover, a native son of Gori.

I need not have bothered myself. I was given archive material never shown before in the West, grim evidence of the terrible slaughter that accompanied the collectivisation of Russian farming. The museum curator, when we came to film, was a model of discreet helpfulness.

'Are you quite sure you have everything you want?'

'Yes, yes. Everything, thank you.'

'All the plugs, cables, lamps? Sure you've forgotten nothing?'

'No, we're quite ready.'

'Right, then I'll leave you now. Just give me a call when you've finished.'

We received not one hostile look, not a single word of criticism, no interference. President Reagan, also called the Great Communicator, suggested, during an address to an audience of clergymen, that the diverse lands of the Soviet Union constitute an 'Evil Empire'. He was evidently trying to express his feelings about it in language which even he could understand. On a more recent occasion, with greater experience if not greater knowledge, he said it was the example of how not to run a country. Margaret Thatcher, describing a Britain without the nuclear deterrent, her beloved weapon of despair, foresaw the British reduced to fighting in the streets like guerrillas. Against whom? The Picts?

The cocksureness of such utterances is even more impressive than their underlying ignorance, and show how far public scepticism still has to go to make politicians think twice before glibly flavouring our food for thought with the condiments of propaganda.

Nobody in his right mind would consider the Soviet Union at the present hour as an experiment remotely approaching perfection. The machine is cumbersome, inefficient, and yet, it would be churlish to deny them a modicum of success in areas in which we have made no serious effort to compete.

We have already touched on the realm of childhood. The standards of theatrical performance and marionette shows specifically for children, their opportunities in sport and cultural activities are certainly more concentrated and organised than they are in countries more reliant on individual initiative. In other words, it is a far from unfortunate destiny to be a child in the Soviet Union. Children are a privileged class.

The same sense of civic pride permeates public transport. Consider, for example, the Moscow Underground, where the stations look like Pompeii before Vesuvius misbehaved. They are the very opposite of functional, and as such they exert an unusual fascination – the spacious spotless platforms, the swift reliable service, the cheap prices. But nearly every Russian city of more than

Filming in Red Square in front of a giant banner with Lenin on it. Preparations are being made for the May Day celebrations.

The Church of St. Andrew, Kiev (1747–67) is one of Kiev's most beautiful baroque churches. It was designed by Bartolomeo Rastrelli, the great master of Russian baroque architecture. He completed drawings for this church in the same year that he began work on budgeting the Great Palace at Petrodvorets.

half a million has its own underground system, equally swift and equally pleasant. And in some cities the feat of engineering is far more considerable than is the case in Moscow. Leningrad is built on marshland, yet the underground was constructed and works just as well.

To travel below the earth past gilded Corinthian columns and statues of Pre-Raphaelite women in scanty dress is strange enough. It is also curious, in Western eyes, to go from a station called Mayakovsky to a station called Gorky and discover on arrival a little shrine, or memorial in stone, to the great writer. I do not recall ever going from Chaucer to Milton on the Circle Line, or from Melville to Mark Twain on the New York IRT.

A flat fare takes you anywhere and I discovered a Las Vegas-like element of chance in the fare collection. I put my coins in the machine and received change equivalent to four more fares. Hit the jackpot, and you can spend your life there. Leaving Karl Marx station, I walked through marble halls and suddenly found myself in Pushkin. The railway tunnel seemed to be duplicated by this gracious promenade, perhaps so that foot travellers could avoid the street-level rigours of the Moscow winter. The whole system seemed to be civilised, or perhaps ancient-civilised, and as clean as a whistle.

Glasnost – 'openness' – has become the trade-mark of Mikhail Gorbachev, although it has been creeping into Russia for some time.

During our expedition to Russia, which began before the arrival of Mr Gorbachev, we shot 77 hours of film taken in various parts of the country. When we left the Soviet Union, the authorities did not ask to see one single foot of it. Out of courtesy we showed them a two hour rough that we had cobbled together, but though they expressed polite interest they kept on looking at the time because they were busy officials with many more important matters to look into. The wave was already in existence, but it is to Mr Gorbachev's credit that he is riding his surf-board so skilfully upon it.

I was in Lithuania just as he took over power. Lithuania is among the most Western in style of the Soviet republics. I asked my local hosts what difference the coming of Gorbachev would make to them. 'Very little,' they replied. 'We are a small country with few people, but we have our own ways. We are not ambitious to influence the affairs of the USSR as a whole, but we are keen to have our say within Lithuania. Russians may come here as our guests. They like to spend holidays here because we are prosperous and efficient, our land is tidy and clean, and we have enough of most things. We do not resent the presence of Russians. They are welcome, they are good for the economy. So, you see, we are a long way down the road to *glasnost* already.'

I know that the nature of society in the year 2000 and beyond lies foremost in many Russian minds. I attended a meeting organised by the Kirghiz writer Chingiz Aytmatov, a visionary and much respected novelist throughout the world. By Lake Issyk-kul, under the overpowering white peaks of the Tien Shan mountains which close off the road to China, Westerners and Russians discussed the problems of our age with great application and good humour, and without any trace of outside 'guidance'.

Among the delegates were Arthur Miller, James Baldwin, Alvin Toffler, Alexander King, the President of the Club of Rome, Augusto Forti of UNESCO, Federico Mayor Zaragoza, the biologist, the Turkish writer Yasher Kemal, Nobel Prize winner Claude Simon, and a handful of others. After we had reached certain conclusions and speculations about the next millenium, we forwarded our slim manifesto to both Mr Gorbachev and Mr Reagan. There was an immediate response from Mr Gorbachev, who asked to see us the day after the conclusion of our meeting. We were told the encounter would be at eleven o'clock sharp, and that it would last precisely one hour. It turned into a very Russian occasion, starting at exactly eleven, with a sensation of count-down before the doors were flung open, and we left a fraction under three hours later. It was fascinating. He began by apologising in advance if anything any of us said provoked him to interrupt us, at the same time begging us to interrupt him if anything he said had the same effect on us. It was

Near Suzdal I travelled in a troika across the empty frozen landscape. Troikas are traditional sleighs which are drawn by three horses, harnessed abreast. Which way to Moscow?

The Tretyakov Gallery, Moscow with a statue of Pavel Tretyakov standing outside. The Tretyakov brothers, Pavel and Sergei, were both collectors of art and in 1892 Pavel donated his collection to the city. This formed the basis of this splendid museum of Russian art.

not the kind of dialogue you expect at the peak of Soviet power, nor indeed at the peak of *any* power.

He demonstrated, more than once, his accessibility and humility. In the course of a major speech in the Kremlin during the subsequent forum of 900 delegates, he stopped suddenly, declaring that he suspected he was speaking too quickly for the translators. His suspicion was confirmed by a shy translator, and so he immediately apologised, said he was prone to let his ideas run away with him, and spoke more slowly from then on, regularly looking at the translators for confirmation that the slow tempo was comfortable for them.

This action illustrated his respect for those who performed more humble functions, but who still played a vital part in the diffusion of his ideas. And as such it was as unexpected as it was intelligent.

On this more intimate occasion, where there were only 14 of us, we were really able to examine the man at close range. Among the surprising sentiments he expressed was that the world is full of debit accounts, and the most pernicious of these was the bankruptcy in new ideas – and this from a country which has been well satisfied with old men and old ideas for a long, long time!

Perhaps even more surprisingly, he said that, after mature consideration, he had come to the conclusion that the individual is the most important element in the world. He immediately held up an admonishing finger, adding, 'This is in no way incompatible with the teachings of Lenin.'

I think we have here the key to the precise nature of his platform. To translate it into Christian terms for easier comprehension, he is reverting to the teaching of Christ, and in so doing he is bypassing Alexander Borgia, the Inquisition and all the men responsible for what could be considered Stalinism in the Church. Before Lenin died, he also instituted the New Economic Policy to stimulate the economy. It was the *glasnost* of the epoch, suppressed by Stalin after Lenin's death because certain people were becoming too rich. The egalitarian convoy had to be animated at the speed of the slowest ship, and if one ship stopped, all of them had to stop, and stagnate for the sake of doctrinaire purity. *Glasnost* is the opening of a window.

It has been attempted often, but has rarely got as far as Gorbachev has already taken it. For the sake of peace, for the sake of Russia, for the sake of all of us, he must be allowed to succeed.

Are communism and capitalism really antagonists? Or is there an unseen line, below which a degree of totalitarianism is inevitable, so that a country may tighten the reins, and pull itself upwards again? Has Russia not risen to that line, perhaps? Is *glasnost* a necessary adjunct to a further advance above the line? And is democracy merely political choice; or is the possibility of choosing between two refrigerators of similar specification and price, or two cars of different colours the first real glimmerings of true democracy? Is it not at that point that men and women irrevocably become individuals, visible as such to their fellow humans, able to argue, to make choices, to have points of view and see those of other people?

The monolith, the stereotype, only lives well below the line.

Children are the inheritors. And one of the things they inherit is the artistic patrimony of the nation, carefully preserved and guarded. Art of all kinds is more than a recreation or a side-line or a frivolity. It is, in Russia, a necessary part of human expression, and it is cultivated as such from the earliest years. As an actor and a playwright myself, I was particularly interested in the children's theatres. Some of these are very large, with an auditorium accommodating up to 1,000 people. Sometimes they are part of a children's complex that may include a reference and lending library for the youngsters, and even a kid's cafeteria. The actors in the children's theatre are nearly all adult, so the classics may be correctly performed. Children do have their own productions with their own casts, but these take place chiefly in the schools. The adult actors tell me that they do not care to stay too long in the children's theatre, for it simplifies their style and they tend to lose touch with their profession. But they regard a short stay as a good training and discipline, and praise the excellent attention and behaviour of the young audience.

In the Soviet Union you come across children's libraries, restaurants and theatres where tastes of all sorts are developed. In this children's theatre in Novosibirsk I watched a performance of Three Fat Men *by the poet Yuri Olesha. In the interval I talked to the audience.*

This Aeroflot jetliner (opposite, above) made a forced landing on the upper reaches of the Volga. Removing the plane proved too difficult so now it serves as a playground for children. The rich, warm red brick of the Kremlin walls and towers at Novgorod (opposite, below). The Church of the Saviour at Kovalyove (above), 1345. This church was almost completely destroyed during the Second World War, which is especially sad because the interior was covered with beautiful frescoes, painted by Serbian artists. It was rebuilt using the original materials and around the outside of the walls a fine white line was drawn to indicate how much damage had been done. It stands alone on top of a hill, about 100 metres from the place where the Red Army stopped the Nazis.

We went to a basketball game in Lithuania between little tots under the age of six. These minute participants brought a strange charm to the game. There is a certain predictability in watching overgrown giants stuff the ball through the hoop with ease, as though dropping ash into an ashtray; but to see tots taking aim from the floor adds another dimension to the contest. I was captivated by one little girl. She was so beautiful, athletic, spry and springy, and diabolically good at the game, that I counted over 50 successful lobs from her tiny hand. Her performance was quite brilliant yet very, very funny. I could hardly refrain from bursting into laughter, a laughter of sheer joyous appreciation.

Old ceremony, old art, old rituals – these are the ballast that Russians consider necessary to carry the ship of state into the next century. Culture is not a market commodity that must sink or swim according to the market values of short-term profit and loss. This is a controversial aspect of Western values. I consider Shakespeare to be a national asset, and his plays have been amortised many times over in the last 350 years. After all, memorials in the street are not asked to pay for themselves. A statue of Richard I, or of Winston Churchill, is not required to pay for its own upkeep, though I have no doubt that a Government infatuated with the market, is even now trying to devise ways of wringing money out of these old stones. Tradition and culture are not merely national attractions which provide profits for the tourist trade. They are part of the living being of a country, and to treat them otherwise is to wound them.

There is some truth in the view that Soviet society operates on suspicion. It is mobilised for action, but action in what direction? The great historical fears which, with some justification, kept Russia in a state of alert tension are now fading under the influence of time, forgetfulness, posterity, tedium. The great question that exercises the West at the moment is how far can Russia afford to relax without breaking the characteristic mould of society that was formed after the 1917 revolution and which, it is believed, cannot be set aside without some new, brutal upheaval.

Lithuania is celebrated for its basketball players, who start learning very early on. I watched some tiny tots play – the Dynamoes and the Torpedoes. The star of the game (above) scored 50 goals.

This Tbilisi tobacco vendor has a flourishing sideline in the sale of pre-revolutionary photographs.

Since I am not an expert in anything, but only a writer and therefore a student of the human heart, I have no compunction at all in giving my opinion. The Soviet Union is ready for a change and will find a way to relax from within itself, despite the constriction of dogma and the deadweight of bureaucracy. Mr Gorbachev, so far, is riding his wave skilfully. The ride is exhilarating and dangerous, with serious consequences if there is a fall, but so far he has kept his equilibrium brilliantly. And I am greatly encouraged by the suspicion and alarm of the Western pundits. For these are the same people who asked questions like – what will follow Mao in China? What will follow Tito in Yugoslavia, Franco in Spain, Salazar in Portugal, De Gaulle in France? The answer, of course, was nothing. As usual, the people were ahead of the pundits in mood and in mental flexibility.

If a liberalisation arrives, what will the Russians make of new freedoms? So often our view of Russia is of a cowed, docile, over-regimented population. Certainly, the levers of Soviet society often work stiffly, with much creaking and jamming. But my view is that the people will have no difficulty at all in putting liberty to work. They are not the subservient people of popular myth. I found hopes and aspirations, argument, political ferment as much a feature of Russian conversation as it is in the West. Russians do not allow themselves to be intimidated. Dissent is a hardy perennial, as Sakharov and those like him have amply proved.

No, the lack of confidence seems to me to be in the West as much as in Russia. I cannot understand why those of us who make modest attempts to promote sympathy, understanding and good humour are branded, by certain organs and certain politicians, as potentially treacherous. Common humanity and good manners, if nothing else, suggest that it might be a better idea to bombard our neighbours with questions and intellectual curiosity rather than with nuclear missiles. To a French journalist who suggested that I was charmed by Gorbachev, I replied, 'The fact that he calls me by my Christian name has no more impressed me than when General de Gaulle, in his goodness, referred to me as Monsieur.'

*Heavy snow adds to the beauty of the museum of wooden architecture at Suzdal (top). A game
of football in the snow outside Rostov (above).*

The freezing Russian winters might feel uncomfortable but they look beautiful. At this time of the year the pigeons rely on the generosity of the visitors at Zagorsk.

I know an American doctor, a professor of the greatest distinction from Johns Hopkins University who has represented UNICEF in the Far East, more especially in China. He is a man of the widest humanity and curiosity, and when he returns to the United States he frequently lectures on all the strange and wonderful things he has

seen in the course of his duties. Invariably, at the end of his lectures, old acquaintances wander up to him to remark balefully, 'Brother, did they ever brainwash you!'

In fact, those who are compelled by circumstances to live in the same place, deriving their view of the world from the same daily newspaper, or watching the same news summary on television, are much more likely to be brainwashed than an inveterate traveller who subjects himself to the rigours of personal experience, with a doggedly open mind.

More important by far than any ideological or material conflict, is a battle in which both the Russians and ourselves are engaged, on the same side. That is the battle for an open mind. We are not brainwashed, neither the professor nor I. We are merely travellers, in quest of an open mind.

So much of the bad feeling, spite and prejudice between Russia and ourselves hinges on the simple question of attitude.

Once, when I was in Leningrad, I came out into the sunlight on a very beautiful late spring morning. One of the first people I saw was an elderly American lady in a black satin pant-suit, her hair held in a snood set with rhinestones. She looked like Juliet's grandmother with a balcony or two in Florida. She was in a very bad mood.

'I hate it here,' she snapped at me expressively. 'O, I just loathe it. I hate Moscow more than Leningrad and Leningrad more than that other place. I don't know why I ever came. It's awful. No one smiles, no one is friendly, they are cold and rude and stubborn. It's just awful, awful. What can you do in a place where no one smiles?'

Just then a middle-aged Russian worker passed. He had a mouthful of ill-fitting gold teeth flanking one lonely gun-metal incisor, and he certainly looked gloomy and barbaric.

'Dobro Utro,' I greeted him. 'Good morning, comrade.'

His face lit up with appreciation and he gave me a radiant smile, the gold around the dud gun-metal tooth shining like the beams from a lighthouse with one defective pane.

'Why did he smile at *you*?' asked the old lady reproachfully.

Well, what can you say?

PETER USTINOV'S RUSSIA:
An Incredible Journey

A personal view of 275 million people. The world's wittiest
host presents that rare thing, a unique video series
that's as much fun as it is fascinating.

Available exclusively in the UK from:
Teltale International, 3 William Street,
Edinburgh EH3 7NG, Scotland
Tel 031 226 3554 Tx 72165

INDEX

INDEX

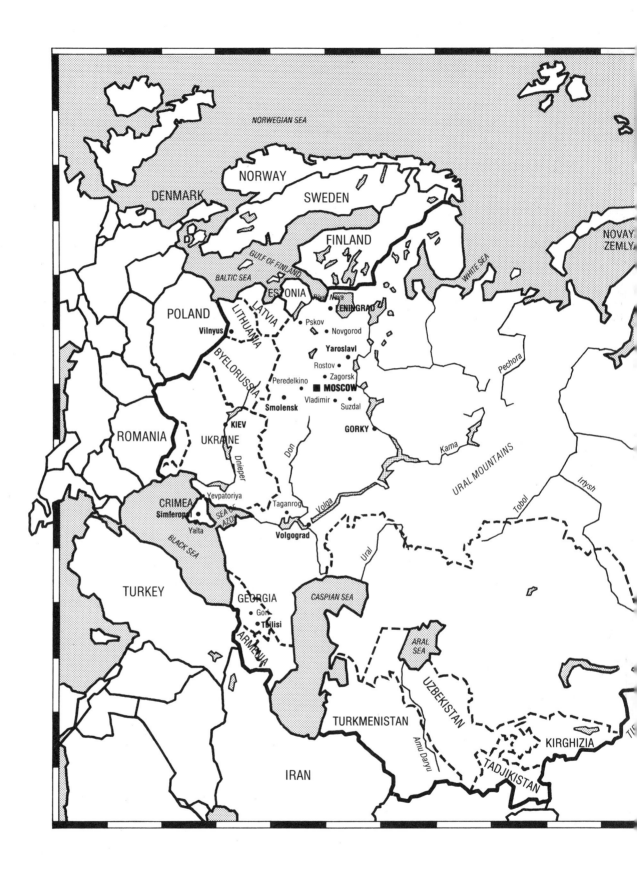